TENNIS:
THE LIFETIME SPORT

Shimon-Craig Van Collie

FOREWORD BY JOHN SUBRIZI

BRISTOL PUBLISHING ENTERPRISES
San Leandro, California

Printed in the United States of America.

ISBN 1-55867-082-3
Library of Congress Catalog Card No. 93-70323

Cover design: Frank Paredes
Photography: John Benson
Illustrator: James Balkovek

Photographs in Chapter 1 of John Suybrizi conducting his Senior Tennis Clinic courtesy of Michael Slear, Brandon Advertising, Myrtle Beach, SC

Basic 10 Flexibility Exercises in Chapter 7 courtesy of U.S. Tennis Association

CONTENTS

ACKNOWLEDGMENTS

Writing a book involves much more work than that of the author alone. I would like to thank the following people for their help, without which this project would have been much more difficult: York Jue, John Powless, Malcolm Clarke, Ken Beer and the other "Super Seniors;" John Subrizi; Paul Roetert and Todd Ellenbecker of the USTA; and the staff at the West Branch of the Berkeley Public Library. Also, my mother Ruth Van Collie, who introduced me to tennis; my wife Katrina, who encourages me to play at tennis and in life; and my son Chai, who makes everything worthwhile.

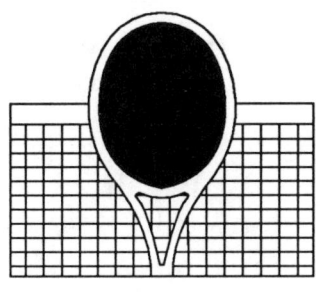

FOREWORD

**BY JOHN SUBRIZI, WINNER OF THE
1992 U.S. TENNIS INDUSTRY AWARD
FOR PROGRAM EXCELLENCE,
INSTRUCTOR FOR HUNDREDS OF
SENIORS ACROSS THE COUNTRY**

Tennis has changed my life. At age 40, I was 35 pounds overweight and very much out of shape. My business was growing, and so was my waistline, a fact I realized one day while playing softball at a picnic. I was soon completely out of breath and felt a pain in my chest. I knew then that I had to do something about my physical condition.

At the urging of my wife Anne, who played tennis when she was young, I picked up the game. Immediately, I fell in love with it. Tennis presented a challenge and the opportunity to get into athletic competition once again.

What amazed me about tennis was that I was a better player at 45 than I was at 40. I was also much better at 50 than I was at 45, and even better when I reached 55. Here I was aging and the quality of my game was improving!

I retired from my job at 55. Having been an active person all my life, I knew I had to do something. At the urging of my son, who thought I would be an excellent teacher, I accepted an offer to teach juniors at a racket club. Always in my mind, however, was the thought that this game should be brought to the masses of seniors to help them improve their physical, mental and overall conditioning. I retired from the racket club to pursue my dream.

Anne, who has become an excellent teacher too, and I have worked together ever since. Here we were, two people in their late 50s, becoming tennis pros, something I would never have believed just a few years before!

We say that tennis may not add one more day to your life, but it will improve the quality of your life while you're living it. Our motto is: "Exercise is the miracle drug of the '90s for seniors, and tennis is their game."

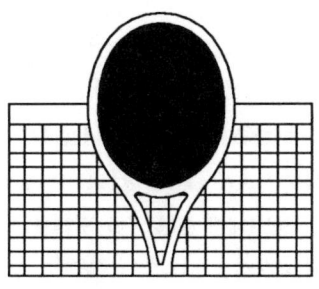

PREFACE

The infamous baby boom generation, as well as the generation which spawned it, are both moving into the senior citizen category. Over 50 million Americans have reached the age of 50 and their numbers will increase over the next 20 years. Many of these individuals are expected to reach the age of 80. Tight budgets in the private and public sectors have increased the popularity of early retirement, which has reduced the number of working men and women over the age of 65. Seniors today have more free time and are better educated, more widely travelled and more affluent than those who preceded them.

Finding fulfilling leisure time activities and exercise programs that are challenging without being too strenuous has become a major search for seniors. Tennis, which can be played at any level for any length of time, is a natural choice. If you can run a few steps and swing a racket, you can play tennis, and you can advance to any level that your desire and physical capabilities will allow. The U.S. Tennis Association now has competitive categories for players into their 80s!

This is not a book about how to play tennis. There are enough books already on the market that cover the basics of forehands, backhands and serves. Instead, this book will attempt to look at tennis from the point of view of a sport that you can play for a lifetime of enjoyment, good health and social interaction. Contained herein are discussions of the benefits of tennis for the mature player, examples of players who have continued to enjoy the sport well into their senior years, some history of the game and equipment, the rules of tennis, suggestions for improving your game, preparations for playing and common tennis problems and how to avoid them. There are also references to other sources for your further education and enjoyment.

Masculine pronouns have been used in this book only as a convention and in no way imply the exclusion of women from the participation or enjoyment of the game of tennis.

Shimon-Craig Van Collie

NOTE: Tennis may not be a suitable sport for those with chronic illnesses or other conditions that may be worsened by unsupervised exercise. Readers should consult with their doctors if they have any doubts about their participation in this sport. Any application of the advice offered in this book is done so at the reader's discretion and sole risk.

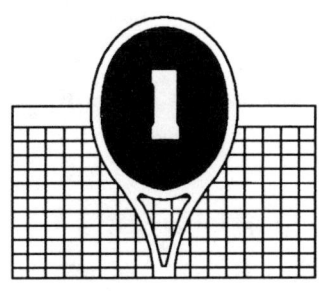

IT'S NEVER TOO LATE FOR TENNIS

In 1992, the USTA presented its Tennis Industry Award for program excellence to one of the leading advocates for senior tennis, John Subrizi, 66, of Stamford, Connecticut. After retiring from his art supply business in 1987, Subrizi and his wife Anne began running free clinics for players over 50. Over the next five years, more than 700 participants, including many novices who had never picked up a racket before, attended Subrizi's free classes, which were sponsored by a number of corporations. The resulting enthusiasm and participation levels have impressed everyone, even Subrizi, who had his doubts about teaching the game to seniors.

A former minor league baseball player, Subrizi took up tennis at 40 as a way to get into shape. He developed to the point where he was teaching juniors at Ivan Lendl's Grand Slam Tennis Club in New York, but found his students' attention span short and his dissatisfaction long. Then he got the idea that it might be more fun and rewarding to teach seniors. Here's what he says about his program:

Everyone Can Learn Tennis

"There has been a great growth in the sport of tennis in the past decade and Anne and I wanted seniors to be a large part of that group. Our programs have proven that absolute beginners who have never played before, even some

John Subrizi, left, explains the proper grip for an effective backhand. Anne Subrizi, who co-teaches with her husband, is second from left.

in their 80s, can learn the game and are now playing on a regular basis. Other seniors who have given up the game early in their lives came back to play the game at a good level. Some of our students have played on a regular basis throughout their lives but who have faulty technique and mechanics to the point of actually injuring their elbows and shoulders. We teach them the proper fundamentals to bring their game to a higher level plus eliminate their physical problems.

"Other tennis teachers joked about the idea when we first talked about it. One of them asked if seniors would drop dead on the court. On the contrary, we get reports that people are in better health. Tennis helps our students' diets, because they will make conscious efforts to correct their food intake in order to improve their tennis performance. We get reports of health improvements such as reductions in blood pressure and cholesterol levels, healthier colons, weight loss, less pain from arthritis and better general physical condition. "

An Antidote to Depression

"We've also found that tennis can be one of the most effective antidotes for depression, a malaise that is not uncommon among seniors who are dealing with their own mortality and that of their contemporaries. A woman who took my first class in 1988 continued coming back for more sessions in the following years. One day, she told me that her husband had passed away the previous winter, and that tennis was the main thing that kept her going that summer.

"Tennis provides mental stimulation. Many of our students say they tried aerobics and swimming, but found these recreations too boring. After a month of tennis lessons, we have to caution them not to play too much and to give their bodies a rest! I had one student who discovered

John Subrizi, second from left, demonstrates a forehand shot for his senior students.

he had to have an artificial hip implant. His doctor told him he'd have to cut out the tennis, because the activity would wear the new hip down. The patient asked how long it would take before that happened, the doctor said between ten to twelve years. My student said that was plenty long enough for him!"

Social Benefits

"In addition to improved health, seniors enjoy the great social benefits of tennis. They now have people in the program with whom they play on a regular basis. Many say it gives them a reason to get up in the morning. I've taught tennis to many age groups in the past, but none has been as eager or as dedicated to learning the game. In addition, they show such gratitude to us and a love for the game. That's why I want to get the word out to the millions of seniors throughout the country that tennis is an ideal game for them."

Never Too Late to Learn

John DiMuro, 75, is one of Subrizi's students. Here's what he has to say about learning to play tennis at the age of 73:

"I was athletic in my youth, but I grew up in New York where there weren't any tennis courts. It looked like fun, but I never played. After selling furniture at Macy's for 48 years, I retired in January 1990. I saw a notice about the seniors program and signed up for the classes. I picked the basics up pretty quickly and was moved from the beginner to intermediate class right away.

"I found that I have the stamina to play for long periods of time without tiring. Now I play two or three times a week for an hour or two each session. We even play in the winter if it's not too windy and the courts are clear. I prefer singles because I like the competition and not having anyone to blame but myself if I do something wrong.

"We have a strong social group too, which helps. Just today I had a 78-year-old woman call me to see if I could play. I also play with younger kids, including my 18-year-old granddaughter. She's pretty athletic and hopes to play in college, but I can play even with her. The last time she visited, she won the first set 6-3 and I won the second 6-4. I was ahead 3-0 when we decided to quit!"

A Senior Champion

Evelyn Roach, 70, is another active participant in Subrizi's program. Unlike John DiMuro, she played tennis before, but her game never really came together until 1992, when she won a silver medal at the 1992 Senior Olympics in doubles. She says:

"I used to live in California and took lessons at the tennis camps. I was always hacking away at tennis, though, and never learned correctly. John keeps telling us he wants us to look like good tennis players. That may sound superficial

John Subrizi, right, offers a personal touch to his teaching. His ability to relate to his fellow seniors makes him a highly successful instructor.

at first, but if you look good, you'll be playing well. And we're also learning to do things that we can do as seniors. We're not trying to run around like teenagers. The net result is that I feel more confident in my game. I play regularly with women who are 20 years younger than me and they ask me questions about playing the game. They're impressed with the improvements I've made in my game. "

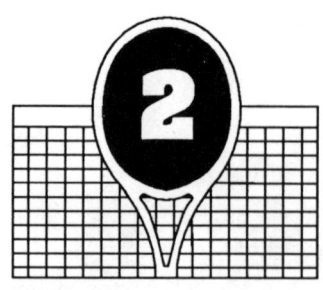

THE ADVANTAGES OF BEING OLDER AND PLAYING TENNIS

It Happens to All of Us

No matter what your level of skill or background of experience, tennis players all have one element in common: every time you step onto the court, whether it's to compete in a tournament, practice your serves or just enjoy a game of mixed doubles, you are older. Many tennis players have reached or surpassed the age of 50, a time when decreasing physical abilities are counterbalanced by increasing wisdom and a broader view of life.

An Enlarged Concept of Winning

"Winning" for a tennis player who has reached the middle years and beyond takes on more meaning than scoring more points than your opponent. Maturity allows you to measure success in many ways: accepting the challenge of competition; recognizing your own improvement in skill; adapting to new partners in both singles and doubles play; and just having fun playing the game. Those who have passed the half century mark take a broader view of life.

The famous cartoonist Charles Schulz, who celebrated his 70th birthday in 1992, argues that Americans have become too preoccupied with keeping score, whether it's in the corporate boardroom or on the athletic field. Rather than worrying about who's winning, we should focus on "the plays, the great goals being scored, the great baskets being made, great overhand shots hit. These are the things that count in sports." With the wisdom of age comes this appreciation of the excitement of sports and not just the outcome.

Tennis as a Social Game and Emotional Booster

Writing about why seniors play tennis for the U.S. Tennis Association (USTA) Senior Tennis Directory, Ronald B. Woods, Ph.D., notes that: "The game of tennis can provide a uniquely satisfying social experience for the senior tennis player. The activity becomes the focus for social interaction between peers and provides the setting for healthy and satisfying relationships with other people. New friends are easily engaged and good friends delight in the pleasure of fun and physical activity that is shared."

Tennis played on a regular basis can enhance self esteem. This is because much of how we feel about ourselves grows out of how we feel about our bodies. Three or four hours of running around a tennis court each week leads to stronger, fitter bodies. You develop endurance. You can control your weight more easily. You are relying on your organs to process your food efficiently in order to provide the energy you need to play the game. Your body takes on a healthy glow from exercise that feels good internally and also projects out to others.

Mastering the different aspects of the game also provides a psychological boost. As you learn each stroke, or as you relearn or refine strokes that you've had for years but with which you have never been totally satisfied, you achieve the emotional rewards of satisfaction and confidence.

Replacing Strength with Wisdom

Tennis teachers constantly remind their students that consistency and control are as much a part of any tennis game as brute strength. Youth tends to favor the latter, when you can bang away at the ball for hours on end, hoping some of them go in enough to win a few points or a match. Nature has been kind enough to replace that strength with wisdom and the accumulated reservoir of experience to allow the older player to know when and where to place the ball, whether or not to hit hard or soft, when to charge ahead full steam and when to hold back and conserve energy.

A Helping Hand From Technology

Technology has also come to the aid of the aging player. Lighter, more powerful rackets can add pace to a stroke that may have eroded over time. Lighter, more supportive shoes give your feet extra protection and resiliency. Studies in peak performance have generated more efficient ways to train and play so that the body and mind get less worn down with extended effort.

RECREATIONAL PLAYERS
WHO ENJOY THE GAME

You don't need to have been a tennis player all your life to enjoy the benefit of tennis. George, a 61-year-old retired telephone company employee, took up the game at 40. He and his wife were looking for a sport they could enjoy together. They found two old warped rackets in the basement of a relative's house and some old, dead balls and started whacking away. "It was a struggle at first," he says, "but a friend of mine at work encouraged me to take lessons. I was agile and had good reflexes, and after a while I got pretty good at it."

George currently plays two to four times a week and stays on the court as many as three or four hours on a Saturday morning. He still enters tournaments. "I've lost some of my speed," he admits, "but I compensate by working on making my strokes more accurate. I used to approach tournament play with the idea that I'd rather win lucky than lose well. That's changed over the years. Now if I get a lot of good shots in and play well, I still feel good no matter what the outcome. Being out on the court is more than just a game."

Life Starts at Forty

Ruth, 72, was another latecomer to tennis, starting at the age of 40 after bearing four children. She found the time demands of golf and other leisurely sports too great, but an hour or an hour and a half on the tennis court provided a good dose of exercise. She still plays five days a week, relying on covered courts in the winter to get her games in.

A dancer in her youth, Ruth quickly grasped the basics of bringing the racket to the ball and covering the court. Given the chance to do it over again, she says she would have sought out better instruction early in her tennis playing days. Admittedly never more than a recreational player, she has nevertheless played on her town doubles team, and she still finds it challenging to match herself against a competitor.

Ruth also adds that the plateau of age has given her a definite advantage over her younger rivals. "I play a craftier game now," she says. "I've also found that younger players tend to get psyched out if they don't win from the start. I've learned that it's not so serious and if I lose early in a game or set, I don't panic."

Improving With Age

There are some who even argue that age not only has psychological advantages, but physiological as well. Mort, 76, has been playing for more than 35 years. He jokes that at his age one of the hardest parts of the game is finding contemporaries with whom to play. He's been blessed with few injuries, even though he plays at least four hours a week. A singles player in his youth, he's switched over to doubles almost exclusively now.

In addition to the increased accuracy of his shots ("I now have a drop shot that is deadly!" he says), Mort has noticed that his ability to anticipate and react to shots has improved with time. "I seem to be able to anticipate just a tenth of a second faster where my opponent will send the ball. I noticed about ten years years ago that I was able to sense whether they were going to hit cross court or down the line. It's quite fascinating."

A Thinking Player's Game

The trade-off between strength and wisdom finds another advocate in Barton Byers, 58, who enjoys the "tennis high" he gets from his weekly games against friends. He often matches up against a 42-year-old who has yet to figure out how to take advantage of his age.

"Most of the time I don't give him the opportunity to wear me down," says Byers. "I always serve to his backhand and I throw up high lobs whenever I need time to recover. I use the lob offensively too. Even if he gets it he's had to run it down. I keep two things in mind: If I keep hitting the ball over the net, I won't lose the point. If I hold serve, I'll never lose the match."

Helping Self Esteem

Pete, 67, runs the machine shop for a large pharmaceutical company and was, by his own admission, "never very coordinated in sports." Six years ago, his company hired Mike Sforzo to be the inhouse tennis and fitness professional. Pete thought he'd give tennis a try. The few first lessons were difficult, but he soon found himself enjoying the game and the exercise. Pete now plays both singles and doubles for up to three hours at a time. "I'm in better shape now than I was at 35," he says. "I just don't get tired out on the court."

Sforzo adds that Pete's case is typical of older players just starting out. They may feel discouraged in the early going. Once past the initial awkwardness, however, they can be, like Pete, hard to stop. "If there's something they can't do on the court," says Sforzo, "I tell them not to worry about it. Everyone, no matter if they're 10 or 80 years old, loves to be challenged and they feel great when they learn something new. When someone like Pete learns to push a younger opponent around the court, he feels like a million dollars."

Pete needed to draw on as much strength as he could a few years ago when his house burned down and he lost his son. Devastated, his interest in work and life in general waned. Sforzo encouraged him to get back on the court where he found ways to help recover his self esteem. "He can retire any time he wants," says Sforzo of his student, "but he'd miss tennis too much. The company also benefits from having him on the job because he has so much experience."

EXERCISE AND
THE AGING ATHLETE

Exercise and its effect on the aging process has been of interest to human beings for thousands of years. The ancient Greek philosopher Hippocrates noted that physical activity might retard aging, and Plato recommended moderate exercise to preserve both mind and body. In more recent times, common opinion dictated that one should "slow down" with advancing age, but recent research has raised the question that maybe the changes often associated with advancing years are more related to slowing down than they are to age itself. Even young people, when they experience periods of inactivity, suffer health problems.

Misconceptions About Exercise and Aging

There are many misconceptions about aging and its effect on your ability to exercise. Among them are:

- the belief that the need for exercise diminishes and ultimately disappears as you grow older
- an exaggerated belief that exercise is risky
- the idea that walking from time to time will yield large health benefits
- an underrated perception of your physical abilities and capacities

Furthermore, those who use these beliefs to slow themselves down tend to experience more health problems, which creates a downward spiral in their well being. Physical inactivity can be more of a factor in the degree and frequency of illness than any other factors, including smoking and being overweight. Those who are inactive also see themselves as being in poor health.

Breaking Attitudinal Barriers

We have lived in a youth-oriented society for many years. These misconceptions about aging athletes have created attitudinal barriers to seniors participating in athletic events. "Old" men or women have not, until recently, been perceived or portrayed as vigorous athletes. Fortunately, those attitudes have begun to change, especially as senior athletes disprove notions about their frailty.

Recent studies have strongly supported the idea that moderate exercise can be a boon to longevity. A 30-year study of 10,000 American men shows that those who participated in sports such as tennis for at least three hours a week had half the risk of dying from illnesses such as heart disease, colon cancer and diabetes than those who exercised infrequently. Those who quit smoking in addition to taking up exercise increased their estimated life span by an average of 2.5 years. They also significantly improved their general health and their vitality.

The famous runner and author James Fixx, in his 1985 book *Maximum Sports Performance*, cited research showing that tennis players in their 70s, including some who have pacemakers to regulate their heartbeat and artificial heart valves, play three or four sets several times a week. Results of the survey showed that the players had few injuries, were able to react to the ball as well as players in their 20s (although their response times were slower) and were extremely motivated to achieve. Tennis provided an important role in both the mental and physical health of their lives.

THE CHANGES OF AGE

This is not to say that certain changes don't occur with age. Perhaps the most significant difference between young and old athletes is the difference in the cardiovascular system. Maximum stroke volume, which is the maximum amount of blood expelled from the heart during heavy work, declines by 15 to 20 percent from early adulthood to old age. At the same time, the buildup of plaque in the blood vessels increases the resistance to the flow of blood. The vital capacity of the lungs falls by as much as 50 percent and the total surface area of the lungs drops by 25 percent as we age. In other words, the older athlete is less able to process oxygen and, thus, perform physical work. It also means less blood circulating through the body, which lowers the amount of oxygen available to the muscles.

Muscular Changes

Muscle mass and strength decline with the passing years. Grip strength and grip strength endurance peak during our early 20s and fall off thereafter, especially after the age of 60. Range of motion in the joints is lost with age, although there has been little, if any, evidence to show that this is due to biological aging. The time needed for muscles to respond increases with age, but this too may be more influenced by disease than by the simple accumulation of birthdays.

Recovery from injury and fatigue takes place more slowly as you get older. Also, you tend to gain body fat with age, and the ability to be aware of whether you're hot or cold also becomes less reliable.

Loss of Bone Mass

Perhaps the most widely known and feared effect of aging on the body is the loss of bone mass and resiliency. The phenomenon can start in women as early as age 35 and progress at a pace of 1 to 2 percent per year. In men, the process tends to start later, around the age of 50, and decline at a slower rate. Osteoporosis accounts for well over a million bone fractures a year, with a tremendous toll in both physical and emotional terms.

THE BENEFITS OF EXERCISE

As outstanding senior athletes such as exercise guru Jack LaLanne and 90-year old Ken Beer, the national tennis champion in the 85-and-over bracket have proven, there is an antidote to the body's deterioration. Its name is exercise, and it can delay or reverse the changes mentioned above. Following are specific ways in which exercise can help maintain vigor and help forestall the ravages of age.

Improve Cardiopulmonary Efficiency

Studies have shown increases in maximum oxygen consumption of 10 to 30 percent as a result of aerobic exercise, as well as a lowering of blood pressure.

Maintain and Improve Muscle Function

Those who remain physically active as they age tend to keep their muscle mass. Aerobic training programs, including tennis, can increase lean body muscle mass and muscular strength, as well as decreasing skinfold fat. Older people can be trained in muscular strength and endurance just as easily as their younger counterparts. After the age of 50, both men and women can gain strength with equal ability.

Maintain a Healthy Metabolism

A loss of muscle mass leads to slower metabolism, and less need for calories to maintain ideal body weight. As they age, however, people tend to keep eating the same way they did when they were younger. To prevent the buildup of fat, you need to reduce your caloric intake and/or keep exercising to maintain your muscle mass.

Increase Flexibility

A 1981 study of participants ranging in age from 65 to 88 who took part in a dance program found that all of their joints had better range of motion after three months. Increases ranged from 8 percent to 48 percent. Care must be taken not to overextend or stress joints. One of the main benefits of exercise is the strengthening of muscles that support the joints, which places less stress on the joints and ligaments. Activity also stimulates the cardiovascular system and can increase blood supply to the joints, which helps keep them healthy.

Improve Neuromuscular Functioning
Exercise helps muscles synchronize their movements and, by enhancing blood flow, helps maintain and prevent the loss of nerve functions in the brain.

Increase Bone Strength
Seniors who exercise can increase the calcium content in their bones and their resistance to fractures. The more that bones are called upon to provide support for muscles in action, the more calcium they demand and build up. Those who don't exercise and/or don't get enough calcium in their diets tend to lose calcium from their bones as it is drawn away for other bodily functions. Researchers believe that the loss of skeletal mass is a major reason for brittleness in older bones, and this is due in part to reduced physical activity. Muscular and vascular stimulation of the bones helps keep them strong.

Help Control Body Fat
Advanced age not only reduces muscle mass but also increases body fat. As you advance from your 20s to 60s, you might gain as much as 20 percent body fat. The danger of this tendency is that excessive fat leads to chronic disease. Fat around the waist, which is more common among

men, is especially dangerous to your health. A low-fat diet and exercise are the best remedies. Recent studies show that a 130-pound tennis player expends 480 calories per hour playing singles, which is more than downhill skiing or jogging.

Help Improve Self Image and Self Esteem

Research reveals that regular exercisers experience less depression than those who are sedentary. The increased flow of blood and higher metabolism that result from running around a tennis court, for example, may inhibit or help process chemicals that are released in the body as part of the stress response. The social nature of tennis —— it takes two to play, after all —— encourages contact with others. Taking tennis lessons as part of a group or being part of an ongoing team or club of tennis players also promotes social interaction.

WOMEN, EXERCISE AND MENOPAUSE

Perhaps a woman's most dramatic passage into middle age is the cessation of her menstrual cycle in her late 40s and early 50s and the hot flashes that accompany this change. The majority of women do not experience severe discomfort from these hot flashes, although those that do can have their normal routines upset by the phenomenon.

Exercise can help alleviate the symptoms of menopause and hot flashes. Researchers believe that keeping your body in shape will enhance the continued production of the sex hormone estrogen during and after menopause. Being physically fit is also believed to help in the reception and utilization of estrogen by the body tissues. Regular workouts, such as tennis, can maintain the sex-hormone glands in top working order.

Handling the Heat

Physically active women are also known to be able to handle heat stress better than women who are less active or sedentary. Women who use their bodies frequently are more adept at regulating their body temperatures through sweating. Extremes of temperature, such as a hot flash, are easier to deal with when your sweat mechanism is fully functional and used to the demands of cooling your body.

Women who are going through menopause and playing tennis should take the normal precautions concerning heat and playing in hot weather. You should wear layers of loose fitting clothing that can be shed easily to keep yourself cool. Drink plenty of cool or cold water before, during and after your time on the tennis court. Avoid playing in the hot part of the day when the sun is highest, or when the heat and humidity are high.

TENNIS AS AN AEROBIC ACTIVITY

Tennis has been seen by some medical experts as one of the lesser aerobic activities. So much time was spent between points walking around or standing still that the sport was not considered a true test of the body's heart and lungs. That myth has been re-examined recently, with the results showing that a game of singles can be a perfectly good aerobic workout.

An article in the May 1989 issue of *World Tennis* magazine pointed to a 1984 study at the University of New Mexico in Albuquerque demonstrating that singles players can, in fact, achieve the required 60 percent of predicted maximum heart rate in the course of a game. Of course, the players are not always in motion because they stop between points to pick up balls or await the next serve. As long as they don't spend too much time doing such non-aerobic activities, the heart rate does not drop significantly to take the players out of the aerobic condition. An hour and a half of such vigorous tennis per week, according to the results of the study, will maintain cardiovascular fitness.

Ways to Aerobicize Your Tennis

There are ways to increase the aerobic aspect of tennis. One obvious way is to run and move more. By doing so, you'll get to your hitting position faster and you can set up for the shot. Move your body into the ball. One of the primary causes of tennis elbow is an overuse of the arm to hit the ball. Power to your stroke comes from moving your body weight into it, not from how fast you can whip the racket around with your arm. Stroke through the ball — keep your racket face going forward as long as possible as you swing (like a paddle going through the water). Bend your legs before you hit the ball and use them to propel you into the shot, especially ground strokes, overheads and serves.

Playing singles will give you more of a work-out than doubles. Playing with six balls instead of the traditional three will keep you hitting longer and spending less time picking up balls. Run to set up for your shots and have your partner hit balls from side to side and short and long so that you have to scamper to retrieve them. You can also play shadow tennis, whereby you imagine that an opponent is hitting you a variety of shots around the court and you have to chase all of them down. This last exercise will not only provide aerobic benefits, but it will help you visualize your form and prepare for an actual game.

Get a Check Up

Before starting any exercise program, of course, you should get a physical check up. The high prevalence of coronary artery disease among aging Americans, both male and female, requires a medical evaluation. For those who haven't exercised much before, or who have been inactive for many years, caution is the operating word when starting any exercise program. Your workouts should be long and vigorous enough to provide stimulation but not to risk injury.

In addition to the benefits of exercise listed earlier, aerobic activity can produce some of these additional health advantages:

- lower the blood pressure in hypertensives
- reduce body weight
- improve glucose tolerance in diabetics
- increase the levels of high-density lipoproteins (which protect against coronary heart disease)
- reduce blood clotting tendencies
- encourage a more health-conscious lifestyle

GETTING READY ON AND OFF THE COURT

Whether you're learning tennis from scratch or coming back to the game after a long hiatus, you can't just walk on to the court and "go full out" for two or three sets. There are skills to learn or relearn. There are also physical demands that tennis makes on your body and you can prepare for them in order to make your experience of the game more enjoyable.

Monitoring Heart Rate

Before you start playing, you need to get checked out by a doctor, of course. You also need to be able to monitor yourself on the court so you know how far you're pushing yourself and when you need to back off.

The American College of Sports Medicine has issued widely used guidelines for a training heart rate. You can compute yours by subtracting your age from 220 to get your maximum heart rate (the older you are, the lower that number will be). Then take 60 percent and 80 percent of that number (multiply by 0.6 and 0.8). The resulting numbers give you the upper and lower ends of your target heart rate zone.

While you're exercising, your heart rate per minute should fall between those two numbers in order for you to receive aerobic benefit. If you've been relatively sedentary for a long time, you'll want to start at the lower end of the scale. If you're more physically fit, or as you become more fit, you can shoot for keeping your heart rate at the higher end.

You'll find after taking your heart rate for awhile that you'll automatically know when you're in your training zone. The exception would be if you're a heart or high blood pressure patient and you need to monitor your heart rate more rigorously.

MAXIMUM/TRAINING HEART RATES BY AGE

AGE	MAXIMUM HEART RATE (per minute)	TRAINING ZONE 60%	80%
50	170	102	136
55	165	99	132
60	160	96	128
65	155	93	124
70	150	90	120

For those over 70, especially those who haven't played tennis before or who haven't exercised much in their lives before, doctors recommend taking a treadmill stress test to establish a baseline maximum heart rate. This test will also reveal any underlying heart diseases that might be a problem. Once you've established your individual maximum target heart rate, you can compute your training zone heart rate and keep track of it while you're playing.

KNOW THE WARNING SIGNALS OF IMPENDING HEART PROBLEMS

Some tennis players will tell you that, if they have to go, they'd rather do it on the tennis court than anywhere else. Ample anecdotal evidence can be found of those players who simply keeled over between games. Of course, we'll never know whether or not the experience fulfilled their fantasies.

For many, if not most Americans over 50, especially men, heart disease or the threat of it is the bogeyman in the closet. For whatever reasons, heart attacks have become frighteningly commonplace, and anyone who says he isn't worried about having one himself is probably not telling the truth. As the work and job-related stresses that contribute to heart disease begin to affect women as they have men for the past half century, it's important to know what the warning signals are. If you or one of your tennis partners begins to exhibit those symptoms, or makes reference to them in conversation, you may be able to avert a more serious medical situation.

The Warning Signals

Some of the warning signs of heart trouble that may exhibit themselves are:

- pain and discomfort in the chest, abdomen, back, neck, jaw or arms. These symptoms may indicate that blood and oxygen are not being pumped efficiently from your heart.

- nausea during or just after a workout.

- unusual shortness of breath during a workout. If you're used to playing a couple of sets without a normal degree of breathlessness (a good aerobic exercise will, by design, make you breath hard) and suddenly you find yourself short of breath, consult a doctor.

- dizziness or fainting, especially during a workout.

- irregular pulse or heartbeats.

CROSS TRAINING TO IMPROVE CONDITIONING

You may even want to start a training program to ready yourself for tennis, or start one concurrently with your tennis lessons so that as you gain skill at the strokes, you'll be in shape to stay on the court after the lesson's over. Any number of activities can help your conditioning, including walking, jogging, climbing stairs, riding a bicycle, swimming, aerobic dancing and rowing.

Fitness isn't something you attain overnight. People who have been active much of their lives will be more likely to adjust well to the demands of tennis. Those for whom tennis is the first sport in their life will encounter many new sensations in those first few weeks, not all of which may be pleasant, such as sore muscles. The important thing is not to get discouraged and to use all your support systems, such as your friends, family, fellow players and medical personnel to keep you moving towards improvement, both in your game and your physical condition.

Hints to Help You

Whether you're playing tennis or engaging in another physical activity to condition yourself for tennis, here are some guidelines to help with your workouts.

Don't Push for Too Much Too Soon

One of the advantages of being over 50 is knowing that the most important thing in life isn't running a mile in less than four minutes or completing an outrageous number of pushups in one set. By now, you've learned a bit about your body and how to pace yourself so that you don't overdo exercise. If you find that the partner you're playing with or the teacher you're working with doesn't respect your limitations, or wants you to do more than you're ready to do, find someone else to work with.

Don't Believe the Exercise Adage "No Pain, No Gain"

Pain is the body's indicator that you should slow down or alter the way you're doing an exercise. For seniors, pain may also indicate a more serious problem than exercise stress, which makes it even more important to pay attention to. Any severe discomfort in the neck or chest, for example, calls for the immediate attention of a doctor.

Keep Your Body Under Control

Flailing about, whether it's on the tennis court or taking a dance class, can set the stage for injury. Wildly gyrating limbs place undue stress on joints.

Maintain Good Form and Posture

"Looking good" is a phrase that has come to denote a false sense of mastery in our society. Yet there is merit to the idea that if you look good — if your movements are graceful and fluid — you will be using your body more efficiently. You also need to check your posture to make sure your spine isn't twisted or misaligned. The keys to remember here are keeping your abdominal muscles contracted, your buttocks tucked under and your knees slightly bent. All three of those adjustments work together to keep your spine in what is called the "neutral" position, which protects the muscles and nerves from stress and allows you to move more efficiently.

Avoid High-Impact Aerobics

Exercise classes where participants jump up and down for several minutes at a time to increase their heart rate can lead to injuries to the shins, calves, lower back, ankles and knees. Since the heyday of this form of workout in the 1980s, exercise experts have developed low impact routines, where one foot remains on the floor at all times and the movements send fewer shock waves up through your feet, legs and spine.

Consider the Quality of the
Air When You Exercise

The reality of modern urban, and in some cases, suburban living includes the presence of automobiles which produce carbon monoxide, sulfur dioxide and other airborn pollutants, including the smog-producing ozone. Symptomatic responses to these pollutants can include chest pain, coughing, throat irritation and difficulty in deep breathing. If any of these are a concern to you, try to schedule your workouts during times when auto activity would be minimized, such as before or after the workday rush hour.

Conditioning Is Not an Olympic Sport

For many people, the thought of "getting in shape" ranks as part of their personal realm of dreaded dictums, others of which include phrases like "losing a few pounds," "getting myself organized" and "fixing the screen door on the back porch." If getting in shape is something you've resisted for 50, 60 or 70 years, this book (or any other) will probably have little impact on your personal lifestyle.

However, here's a thought that may prove liberating in the arena of physical fitness: it doesn't have to be a lot of hard work. You don't have to pack yourself off to the gym five days a week, or plunge into the pool for an hour a day. There are simpler ways to start working your body, ways that will, over a period of months and years, make a difference in your overall physical condition. They will also complement your tennis game by giving you a healthier base from which to work.

Look for Ways to Exercise

While much of the 20th century was spent looking for ways to save human beings from physical labor, now is the time to start looking for ways to reintroduce some physicality to your daily life. Some obvious examples are walking or riding a bike to work, to the store or anywhere else where you can leave the car behind. Don't rely on elevators and escalators totally: if you have to go up ten flights, take the elevator halfway and walk the other half. Descend using the stairs as well. If you're early for an appointment, take a walk around the block. Shopping malls are great places to stroll, especially if you're concerned about personal safety. There are even groups that walk en masse around malls for exercise.

Exercises Are Where You Find Them

Take exercise breaks during the day. If you're working at a desk, stretch every half an hour. Get up and walk around. Target a certain number of stretches or exercises, like knee bends or push-ups, and divide them up into segments during the day. If you're working around the house, find ways of relying on your muscles instead of a machine to perform certain tasks, like mowing the lawn or cleaning the floors.

Exercise in Front of the Television

Time in front of the television can be spent exercising as well. Design a workout routine, including stretching and strength building exercises, to last througout a 30-minute program. If you have an exercycle, put it in front of the tube and pedal away during your favorite sitcom.

Research shows that moderate exercise, or what could simply be called an active lifestyle, can produce some of the same kinds of benefits that can be gained from vigorous aerobic exercise. One study showed that men who regularly perform such activities as gardening, walking, household chores or even bowling for an hour a day have stronger hearts and less risk of heart disease. The same kind of conditioning effects from moderate exercise would also help prepare your body for tennis and help keep your level of fitness once you start playing the game.

Bathroom Tennis

Being a game that is as much mental as it is physical, tennis can be practiced just about anyplace. In 1978, Alan Boltin, a tennis teacher, published a book called *Bathroom Tennis*. Boltin advised a total understanding of the game on the mental, physical and emotional levels. To help people gain this mastery, he devised an eight-minute routine involving stretching and warming up (done before taking your daily shower), visualization (done during your shower) and movement (done after your shower). Part of his plan called for readers to visualize themselves playing brilliantly. "You can't lose in the bathroom!" he writes.

WARMING UP

Many of us imagine that the best way to start a workout is to stretch our muscles. Current thinking suggests, however, that stretching cold muscles may be counterproductive because they lack elasticity. Tests on animal muscles and tendons show that you need more force to tear tissue after it has been warmed up than before.

You can warm up your muscles first by walking, riding a bike, jogging or climbing stairs. Five or ten minutes of this type of activity will perform several beneficial functions, such as gradually increasing heart rate and blood flow, raising the temperature of muscles and connective tissue, and improving muscle function.

By warming up first, you'll also be reducing your chance of injury. When you try to push your body into strong exertion without preparation, you run the risk of abnormal heart rate and inadequate blood flow to the heart, along with changes in blood pressure. These risks are especially dangerous for senior athletes.

changes in blood pressure. These risks are especially dangerous for senior athletes.

Use Court to Your Advantage

Why not use the tennis court itself to choreograph your warm up? For example, you can jog from the baseline to the net on one of the sidelines, then backpedal to the service line and shuffle sideways to the middle of the court. At the centerline, jog forward to the net again and backpedal to the service line again. Continue to shuffle across to the opposite sideline from where you started and repeat the cycle. At the same time, you can dribble a ball with your racket, either by bouncing it on the court or up into the air. This added exercise will warm up your wrist and arm as well as improve your racket control.

Adjust Your Warm Up to the Conditions

Your warm-up periods can be climate specific. In warmer weather, for example, your body will already be fairly loose and warm, so you don't need to spend as much time in this phase. In cold weather, you may need to spend a few more minutes to create a light sweat, which is a good indicator that you've warmed up enough to start stretching. When it's cold, you can warm up indoors before going outside. Conversely, after a cold weather workout, you can warm down indoors to prevent chilling.

STRETCHING

Once you've warmed your body slightly, it's time to stretch, which is an art in itself. Many older adults grew up in the era when stretching involved short, bouncy movements, such as toe touches or lunges. Like many other phases of sports physiology, these methods have proven to be, in many case, ineffective and sometimes even damaging.

In his excellent book *Stretching* (which includes a special section on tennis-specific stretches), author Bob Anderson notes that the muscles protect themselves from stretching too far or too quickly by contracting. This reflex is similar to what happens when you touch a hot stove: you automatically pull back from the heat. Cold muscles that are stretched beyond their limits or that are overstretched by bouncing will respond with the stretch reflex, making them even less supple than when you started stretching!

Easy Stretching

The way to avoid the stretch reflex is to begin with an easy stretch, one which produces mild tension. Hold the stretch for a slow count of 10 to 30. As the mild tension eases, you can take the stretch a little further until you experience mild tension once again. Again hold the position for a count of 10 to 30. At no point do you want to take the stretch to the point where it becomes painful.

Don't Forget to Breath!

Breathing during stretching is crucial. Dancers and yoga practitioners talk of breathing into the stretch. Imagine that as you draw in air, you send it directly to the muscles which you're lengthening. You can also use the image of filling your muscle with the air that you're breathing, and then deflating it as you exhale. After you release the stretch you should feel a mild warmth and a looseness that indicates the muscles are ready to go to work.

Stretching Before and After Exercise

Todd Ellenbecker, the clinical director of sports medicine at HEALTHSOUTH Sports and Rehab in Scottsdale, Arizona and a member of the U.S. Tennis Association's Sports Science Committee, advocates stretching both before and after working out. "After playing tennis or working out," he says, "your muscles are more elastic. Stretching at that point helps maintain your flexibility and decrease the soreness you might feel the next day."

Delayed-Onset Muscle Soreness

The soreness to which Ellenbecker refers is not uncommon when you start a new sport and/or overextend yourself. You may feel tired but pain-free when you walk off the court, but the next day or the day after, you'll wake up with incredible muscle discomfort. This delayed-onset muscle soreness isn't permanent but may last as long as a week or more. Most often, the condition results from an activity where you are lengthening a muscle and putting stress on it at the same time. An example would be stretching one leg out to reach a wide shot off to one side of the court and stopping short so you can return to get the next shot.

Stretching after play may help prevent this type of soreness, but even more important is the physical training you've done beforehand. If you practice making lunges to the side and recovering and do it under control, you can get your body acclimated to the movement before you try it in the heat of competition.

Dealing With Sore Muscles

Once you've become sore, rest is one of the best remedies. That doesn't mean inactivity, however. Working your muscles lightly, such as walking or swimming, will stimulate the recovery process more than just sitting around. You'll also be better prepared to pick up the pace once the pain's subsided.

U.S. Tennis Association Basic Stretches

As part of its efforts to help tennis players enjoy the game and the health benefits that go with it, the U.S. Tennis Association recommends ten basic flexibility exercises. The association advocates performing these stretches daily, whether you're playing tennis or not.

The USTA also suggests a general warm up period of five to ten minutes where you jog slowly or perform easy jumping jacks to the point where you start to perspire. Perform stretches for the areas that are particularly tight, and don't forget to stretch both sides of your body. Then go out and play tennis. Afterwards cool down by doing all ten of the following exercises to help keep the muscles supple and decrease soreness.

Other safety tips for stretching:

- Use slow, smooth movements when you stretch and coordinate your breathing with your movements. Exhale as you move into a stretch and each time you move deeper into the movement. Check your body for areas of tension as you are stretching and let them relax.

- If a stretch hurts or you feel a burning sensation, you're extending too far. Ease off slightly until the pain subsides and hold that position.

- Stretch to your own limits, not to someone else's or to some preset maximum stretch.

U.S. TENNIS ASSOCIATION
THE BASIC 10 FLEXIBILITY EXERCISES
(Reprinted with permission of the USTA.)

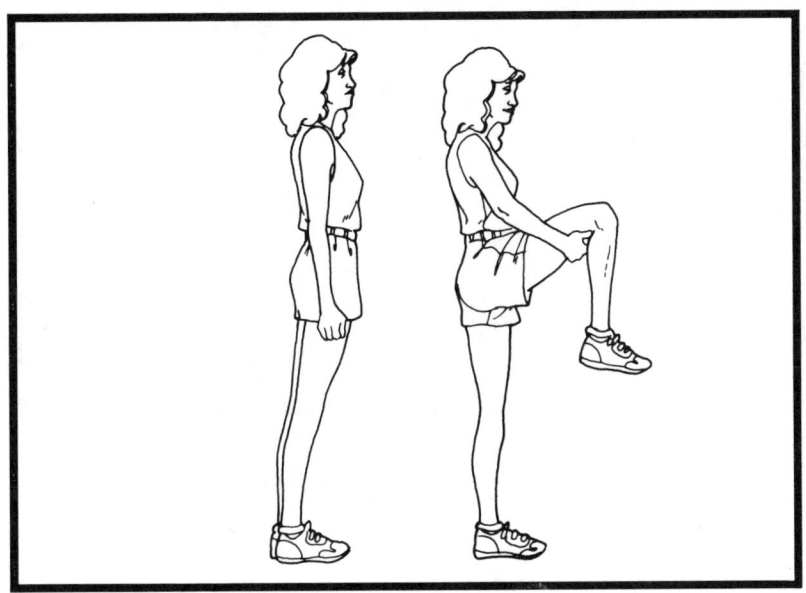

1. Knee-Chest Flex

In a standing position (you can stand with your back to a wall or fence for support), raise one knee and grasp the back of your thigh just above the knee. Slowly pull the knee to your chest and hold the leg in that position. This stretch helps loosen the muscles of your buttocks and your back.

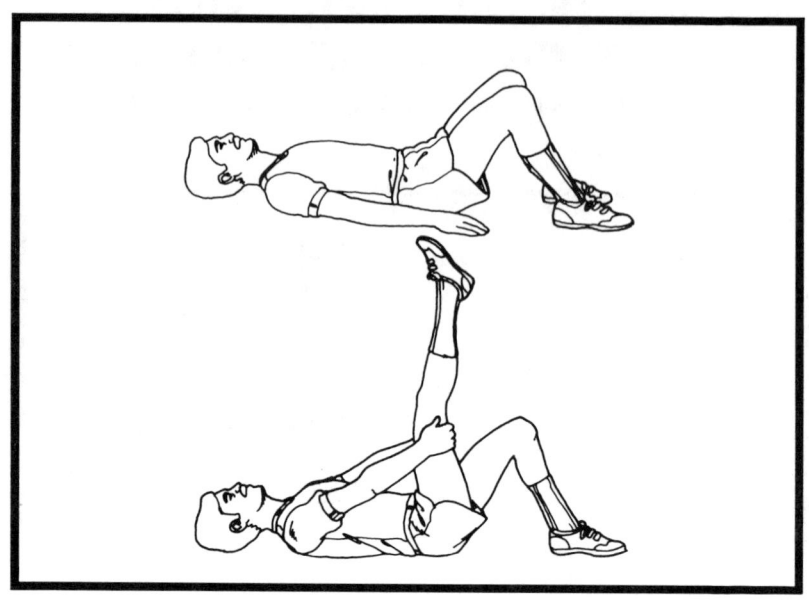

2. Hamstring Stretch

Lie on your back with your arms at your sides and your feet drawn up so your soles are resting flat on the ground. Straighten one leg and raise it towards your upper body. To increase the stretch, use your hands to gently pull your leg closer to your torso. You will feel the stretch along the back of your thigh. By pointing your toe toward your face at the same time and extending your heel, you can stretch your calf at the same time.

3. Figure-4 Hamstring Stretch

Sit with one leg extended and the other drawn up so that your foot touches or is near the inner thigh of the extended leg. Looking down at your legs, you'll see an inverted 4. Keep your back and neck straight and bend forward from the hips toward the extended leg. Again, to stretch the calf as well, point your foot toward your face and extend your heel.

4. Spinal Twist

Sit with your left leg extended and with your right leg bent. Place your right foot on the ground outside of your left knee. Then take your left arm and cross it over the right knee, bringing your elbow outside of the knee joint if possible. Slowly turn your shoulders and head to the right, using your right hand on the ground behind you to keep your spine upright. Extend the stretch by turning your head to the right and look over your right shoulder.

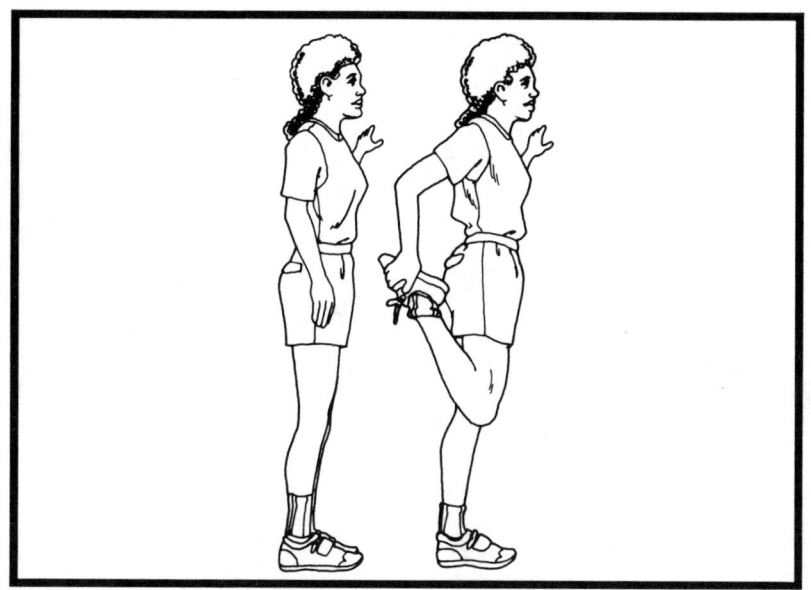

5. Quadricep Stork Stretch

Stand on one leg, using the arm on the same side as the standing leg for support if you need it. Bend the opposite knee and grasp the ankle. Keeping your back flat and your buttocks tucked under, bring your knee down as far as you can. Try to point it towards the ground. Do not point the knee out to the side or twist it.

6. Groin Stretch

Stand with your legs spread more than shoulder distance apart and your toes pointed forward. Place one hand above your knee and the other hand on the opposite hip. Slowly bend the knee your hand is on until you feel a stretch in the groin area. Deepen the stretch by rolling your weight onto the inside of the foot of your straight leg.

7. Hip Stretch

Stand with your right hand on the wall with your weight on your right leg. Cross your left leg in front of the right. Gently push your right hip toward the wall. To increase the stretch, stand farther away from the wall.

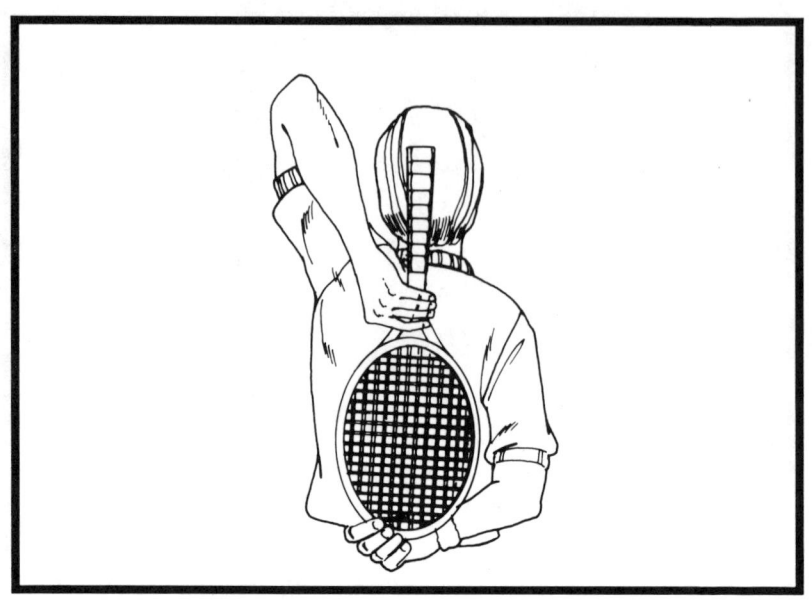

8. Shoulder Stretch

Put your racket behind you so that your upper hand is holding the grip and the lower hand is holding the top edge of the frame. Slowly pull the racket down with the lower arm, bringing your upper elbow to your ear and pointing it to the ceiling. Then slowly pull up with the top arm, pointing the lower elbow to the floor.

9. Calf Stretch

Stand arm's length away from and facing a wall or fence. Put your hands on the wall for support. Step backwards one foot length with one leg. Keep your back knee straight and your heel on the floor. Both feet should be pointing forward. Bend your forward knee and lean your trunk forward. Do not arch your lower back. You should feel the stretch in the calf just below the knee of the extended leg.

To move the stretch down into the Achilles tendon and the heel, slightly bend your back leg and raise the heel an inch or two off the ground. Lean into the wall.

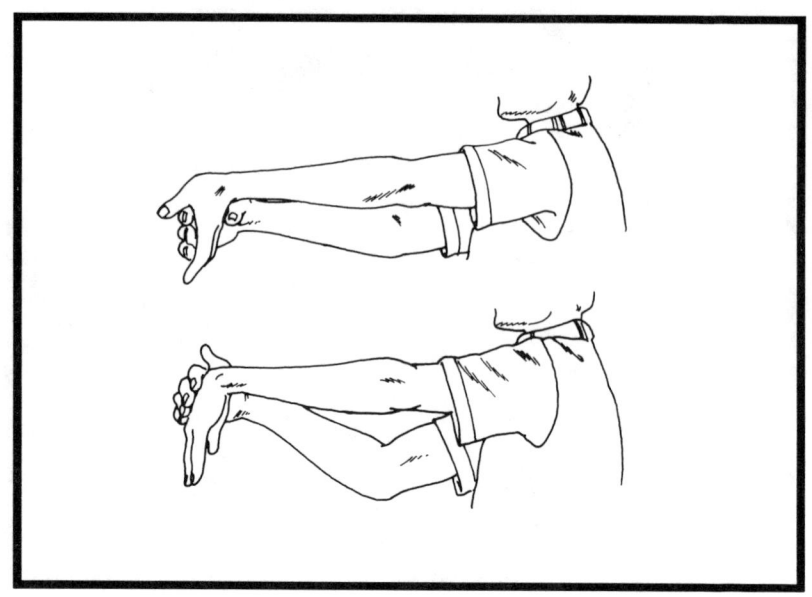

10. Forearm Stretch

Extend one arm out straight in front with the elbow straight and the palm facing up. Use the opposite hand to gently stretch your wrist back in extension. Then turn your hand over so that the palm is facing down and gently stretch your wrist downward into flexion.

PLAYING IN THE EXTREMES

HOT WEATHER WORKOUTS AND FLUID REPLACEMENT

You may have grown up believing the notion that drinking water or any other liquid during a workout was verboten. In his book *Quality Tennis After 50...Or 60...Or 70...Or...*, septuagenarian author Peter Schwed recalls that in his youth he believed that the ingestion of water during a match would cause a debilitating stitch in his side or worse. On a blazing hot day, the most he and his fellow players would consume was a mouthful of warm --- never cold --- water with which they would gargle but not swallow.

A Radical Change

Medical opinion about the intake of fluids has completed a 180° swing since those days. Not drinking water during tennis is considered as harmful as drinking it was 40 years ago! The turnabout is now based on scientific research, which shows that physical activity which produces sweat drains water from the body. Sweating cools the body, but if you run out of coolant, just like your car, you'll overheat. The main symptoms of hyperthermia, as this condition is known, are headache, light-headedness, dizzines, confusion, disorientation, clumsiness, nausea, muscle cramps, hallucinations and either excessive sweating or no sweating at all. Needless to say, this condition can be a serious health threat, even to those who are in excellent shape, with possible damage to the major organs, particularly the kidneys.

WAYS TO AVOID HYPERTHERMIA

Acclimatize Yourself

If you're taking a vacation to a Southern state, don't run out on the tennis court for three sets as soon as you deplane. Start your workouts slowly and pace yourself in terms of exposure to the heat and humidity. It may take as long as two weeks for your body to fully adjust and for you to be able to perform the way you did in cooler conditions.

Keep Yourself Hydrated

Drink eight ounces, or one cup, of cool or cold water before you start playing, even if you're not thirsty. Research shows that cold water gets into your system sooner than warm. The stomach can only absorb a finite amount of water in a given amount of time, so flooding your system won't be as effective as continually taking smaller amounts of water over the duration of your workout. If you're out on the court longer than 30 minutes, start drinking a cup of water about every 20 minutes or so to keep yourself hydrated. Keep drinking water after you've stopped exercising until your body returns to normal.

Plain water is adequate when it comes to keeping yourself hydrated. Some high visibility athletes have popularized specially formulated sports drinks in the last few decades. These drinks promise to replace sodium and potassium lost through sweating and to supply carbohydrates in the form of sugar. The problem with the latter is that it can slow down the absorption of the fluid in your body. Sports drinks can also leave you feeling bloated. If you want to use them, try diluting them, or put a slice of lemon or some fruit juice in your water jar to add a little taste.

Wear Proper Clothing

Always wear a hat in hot, sunny weather. You can don a visor, which will protect your eyes from the sun's glare and, if it features an absorbent headband, will keep the sweat from running down into your eyes. A visor will not protect the top of your head. If you are sensitive to extreme exposure to sun or you have less hair on top of your head to protect from the sun's rays, you'll probably want a full cap.

Sunglasses can be helpful in bright sunlight, although some players find that the dark lenses cut down their ability to see the ball while it's in play. Glasses also have the unpleasant tendency to fog up if you're sweating up a storm, so have a wipe cloth on hand to clean them off between points.

Sunscreen provides protection from the sun's harmful radiation and also helps prevent suffering from sunburn. Apply the gel or liquid liberally to any exposed skin.

Loose-fitting, porous clothing promotes air circulation. Your body's sweating mechanism shouldn't be hampered by layers of clothing, even if you think you can "sweat off a few pounds" on the court. Any weight you lose by this method will soon be regained, and, in hot, humid weather, you increase your chances of overheating.

Sponge Off

Rub a wet towel or a cloth dipped in cold water on exposed portions of your body. This will bring sensory relief and help lower your body temperature.

COLD WEATHER WORKOUTS

Once you've been bitten by the tennis bug, it may be hard to not play when the weather turns cold. Fall, winter and spring tennis is also more attractive because the fair weather players will be indoors and the courts tend to be more available. There's no reason not to play cold weather tennis, providing the court surface is safe — no water or ice to make footing treacherous — and you follow these health guidelines.

Get Your Doctor's Okay

Make sure your doctor clears you for exercising in cold weather. The cool air you breathe into your lungs can cause problems for those with angina, asthma or high blood pressure. Wearing a scarf or a ski mask that covers your mouth and nose will help warm up the air before it reaches your lungs.

Layer Your Clothing

As your body temperature rises, you'll begin to sweat. To prevent overheating and the buildup of sweat, which will rapidly cool if there's a break in the action and after you finish playing, you need to peel off one or more layers. Thin, loose-fitting clothing is the best, because you can regulate your temperature more precisely.

Wear a Hat

You lose most of your heat through your head, so this is another way to regulate your body temperature. A baseball cap might work in temperate climates, but for those cold northern days, you'll probably need a wool cap or one that folds down into a face mask in case the wind picks up.

Hydrate Yourself

You need to replace fluids just as you would on a warm day. The sweat you produce and the work your body does to heat and moisturize the cold air you're breathing demand the intake of fluids. Avoid caffeine and alcohol, both of which tend to dehydrate your system. Try hot water, herbal tea or soup broth instead.

Stay Warm

If you begin to feel the cold after you've shed a few layers, put one or two pieces of clothing back on. If the pace of the game slows down too much, keep moving or suggest to your partner(s) that you pick up the pace.

Know the Warning Signs of Frostbite and Hypothermia

Numbness, itching and a prickly sensation are the first indicators of frostbite, as is a white or pale discoloration of the skin. These symptons usually appear on your extremities, such as hands, ears, toes and face. (Men should also beware of penile frostbite. Ouch!) Shivering is the first step to hypothermia, which lowers the core temperature of your body. As the condition advances, you become weak and your reflexes slow down. Dressing properly and monitoring yourself (and your partners) is the best prevention against these problems.

Protect Yourself From the Sun

Even on winter days, sunlight can be a problem, especially as it bounces off snow or ice. Wear sunglasses if you can and don't forget your sunscreen!

Playing With a Cold

If you catch a winter cold or flu (or even if it's summertime), you should think twice about going out to exercise. If your symptoms are mostly in your head — sneezing, runny nose, sore throat — you can probably exercise without doing further harm. If, however, you have a fever, spend the afternoon in bed or resting at home. An infectious fever can cause hyperthermia and cause damage to your heart. It's better to let your body temperature return to normal and stabilize for a couple of days before you attempt any vigorous exercise again.

IMPROVING YOUR GAME AND MAINTAINING MOTIVATION

TAKING LESSONS

All other factors being equal, the best way (and some would say the only way, although that may be too pedantic) to improve your game is to take lessons. While just playing tennis will improve your fitness, it can also perpetuate weaknesses in your game. Without the trained eye of an observer to help, you will continue hitting the ball or moving around the court in ways that are familiar. This is especially true if you play in matches, where the temptation to experiment (and possibly improve) often succumbs to the habit of sticking to your strengths and not risking defeat or embarrassment.

Quality instruction can be found at any number of locations, including tennis clubs, schools and universities, tennis camps and community service groups, such as the YMCA and town or city recreation departments. A good instructor will analyze your game and work on improving your weak points. You will not only receive verbal and perhaps video feedback, but you will have motor skill drills to work on after or between lessons.

Differing Philosophies for Seniors

Gil Howard, a ranked senior player and head of the Gil Howard Tennis School in Daly City, California says that his approach to teaching older players doesn't vary significantly from any other age group. He tends to de-emphasize the serve and volley type of game for senior players, simply because most of them aren't going to want to be continually running around the court.

"We might teach them to come to the net once in a while as a surprise tactic," says Howard, "but for the most part we concentrate on the placement of serve and anticipating the next shot. The principles of where to hit the ball and where to move on the court are the same for all ages."

Not all instructors agree with the deemphasis on serve and volley, especially since most older players gravitate towards playing doubles where these techniques can be very useful. John Subrizi, for example, spends considerable time with his more than 50 students working on volleying and approach shots. "We teach them advanced doubles, where both players come to the net after the serve," he says.

By focusing on hitting the ball before the first bounce, players gain racket control and confidence. Subrizi teaches several variations of the volley, including the straight volley, the drop volley and the snap volley (where the motion of the wrist gives the shot extra power). "Once a player learns how to hit the ball while it's still in the air," adds Subrizi, "he becomes dangerous."

Private or Group?

You can take lessons in private or as part of a group. Both have their advantages. Working alone with an instructor, you can zero in on your particular weak points. This special attention will cost more money, but the customized recommendations and drills may make it worthwhile. Group lessons cost less and you can expect to receive less personal attention. However, watching others work on their strokes can shed light on your own. The contacts you make with other students can also create new partnerships and friendships on and off the court, especially since others in your class or group will probably be playing at a similar skill level.

No matter which approach you take, your instructor should provide you with the basics of good instruction: an enthusiasm for the game of tennis and for helping you progress; the ability to make you believe in your abilities and your capacity for progress; and the willingness to answer your questions, no matter how simple or silly they may seem.

Other Teaching Aids

Books and videos are available to help those who want additional education materials. Tennis magazines run ads for instructional material and retail outlets often have several of each for sale. Other sources are libraries and college athletic departments. As with the acquisition of any skill, reading and studying images will help you integrate the various elements of the game. Be wary, however, of adopting the style or stance of the latest 20-year-old phenomenon whose game is based on young, strong muscles and plenty of hormonally-induced stamina!

ARE TWO HANDS BETTER THAN ONE?

While playing with two hands on the racket is not new to the game, the recent success of some top professional players has made the double-fisted approach more popular. The grip is also relatively easy to learn and provides additional power and accuracy, attributes that are sometimes harder to achieve with the one-handed version.

Those with weak backhands, or who lead with their elbows in the backhand (a habit which can lead to tennis elbow), are good candidates for the two-handed stroke. Newcomers to the game, since they don't have an established way of swinging the racket, can pick up the stroke relatively easily as well.

As mentioned, the advantages of a two-handed backhand (or forehand) are increased pace and control over the shot. By using both arms, you've doubled your strength and you've taken some of the strain off the elbow. The second hand helps you guide the racket, and therefore the ball, with more accuracy and allows you to make last second adjustments in the direction of the return. High bouncing balls, which are often returned defensively by one-handers can be attacked with more authority. Imparting topspin (where the ball rotates forward and tends to stay in the court even when hit hard) is easier with the two-handed shot.

For those who are one-arm dominant, learning to use two can be a challenge. "We find that women can learn the two-handed backhand more easily than men because they're more flexible," says instructor John Subrizi.

Two-Handed Limitations

Two-handed shots have their limitations. Setting up for wide shots where you have to reach for the ball can be more difficult when you have to extend both arms. Likewise, low shots can be hard to reach.

Making the transition from baseline shots taken with two hands to volleys which are more properly hit with one hand also presents some difficulties. One-handers tend to have more "touch" on the ball and have the ability to vary the spin on the ball with more ease.

YOU DON'T HAVE TO BE ON THE COURT TO WORK ON YOUR GAME

Even though your game may be social or recreational, you can benefit from watching those who play competitively and professionally. Judith, 56, lives in New York City and has been playing once a week for the past 25 years. She finds watching tennis, either on television or going to the matches at the U.S. Open every fall in nearby Flushing Meadows, benefits her game afterwards. "When I watch good matches," she says, "I tend to internalize what the players do and I play better."

Keeping Your Eye Off the Ball

As children, you learned by watching your parents and others. That skill is still available, as Judith says, and can be a valuable and rewarding part of your tennis game. You will, in the course of your lessons, playing with friends or watching matches on television, see effective players and the ways that they use their bodies. The trick is not to watch the ball in such situations, but to observe the players as they set up to hit and how they move around the court as they prepare for the next return. It takes some practice, but you'll get much more visual information about how to play the game by keeping your eye off the ball instead of on it.

In his landmark 1974 book *The Inner Game of Tennis*, W. Timothy Gallwey described a tennis lesson he once gave where, instead of filling up his student's mind with endless directions ("Shift your weight...bring your racket back earlier...lift your follow-through...") he simply demonstrated a proper forehand several times. He asked the student to get a visual image of the stroke and then try it himself. The result was a picture perfect swing!

Mirror Drills

By simply standing in front of a mirror, with or without your racket, you can imitate advanced players, or you can practice the techniques that your teacher has presented to you. The mirror will give you immediate feedback as to how you're holding your racket and how you're stepping into the ball. You can begin to correlate the internal sensations and how they look when externally expressed.

Visualizing

Visualization, which involves using your mind to go through the motions of tennis, is also another effective self-teaching aid. Sports researchers have found that mentally rehearsing your game, seeing it in all its component parts and grooving it into your brain cells, can help your actual performance.

MAINTAINING MOTIVATION

Anyone who has lived past the age of 50 knows that starting a new program, whether it's physiological, psychological or philosophical, can be an exciting time. You see a goal you want to achieve, such as being in better shape, losing weight or having a more positive outlook on life. You are flushed with enthusiasm for the new activity and plunge full ahead signing up for classes, buying equipment, reading books and magazines and talking with friends. Your ability to stick with the program, though, depends on one or more of the following seven factors.

1. Get Good Instruction

Picking the right person to guide you through the learning, or relearning, steps can make the difference between early failure or long term success and satisfaction. One of the advantages that John Subrizi has in his classes for seniors, for example, is that he himself is a senior. His students can relate to him as a peer who knows about what life brings for those who are retired or who have begun to feel the affects of aging.

2. Learn How to Deal With Injuries

Tennis involves using your body to position yourself on the court and to swing the racket from many different angles and at different speeds. The game has been described as a series of emergencies, each of which you handle as quickly as possible. From head to toes, your body is involved in the game and it will not recover from bruises and strains as rapidly as it used to. Knowing how to deal with those problems, either from your own past experiences or with the help of medical or physical therapy personnel, can maintain tennis as an enhancer to your health instead of a detractor.

3. Create Time to Learn and Practice

Like any skill, tennis takes awhile to gain competence. Unless you are very gifted, you won't just pick up a racket and hit away like the professionals you see on television. Patience and commitment are necessary to begin to learn the strokes and the strategy so that you can begin to enjoy the game.

4. Keep the Program Interesting

If you play the same people at the same time and the same place each time, chances are you will lose interest after a while. That's why being part of a tennis group can be helpful, where you can meet and play different people. Each new opponent will bring a new set of skills against which you must adapt. Your mind and your body will be forced to expand their repertoire, and those types of challenges will continue to make the game exciting.

5. Vary Your Workouts

For the newcomer to tennis and the veteran, tennis can become an obsession. Not unlike their grandchildren, senior tennis players sometimes become fixated on the game and want to play it all the time. Such enthusiasm is great, but consider pacing yourself a bit and perhaps mixing tennis up with other physical activities, such as swimming, bike riding, walking, jogging or dancing. The concept of cross training or alternating sports on a regular basis injects a freshness into each activity and also forces you to use different parts of your body in a more well-rounded fitness program.

6. Mark Your Progress

We all need encouragement, either external or internal. You may, in the course of the first several months of playing tennis, feel that you're not getting anywhere. You may only see how far you have to go rather than how far you've come. Finding a yardstick to measure your progress can be crucial to your continuing interest. That yardstick can be another player with whom you can match yourself over time to see how you're doing. Of course, he or she may be progressing in their game as well, in which case you may not notice a better score for yourself but a higher, more exciting level of play.

Another indicator could be your instructor, whom you visit at different intervals to check your progress and iron out kinks in your game that may have developed. Also, the age of the ubiquitous video camera also allows virtually anyone to become a self coach. Have a friend shoot some tape of you on the court. Watch it to see how you look. Then repeat the same process six months or a year later and see what the differences are.

7. Overcome the Opinion of Your Family and Peers

If you are someone who has never played tennis and one day you start taking lessons, those who are closest to you will probably wonder what's going on. People tend to resist change, and if you begin to show signs of getting in shape or simply express enthusiasm for something about which they know little or nothing, it can be threatening. Even if you have played tennis before, but are taking it up again, the time you spend on the court or conditioning yourself to play can be seen as a threat to your relationships. You may have to spend some time winning your dear ones over to the program. Let them know that you're not taking anything away from them and that they will benefit from a healthier and more vigorous friend or spouse.

KEYS TO SUCCESS

The emphasis of this book is not on how to win at tennis, but how to make tennis a winning experience. For many players, the two are synonymous. We live in a very competitive culture, and we like to see ourselves as winners at whatever we do. The advantage with being over 50 is that the concept of winning expands with time. You may lose a match, but if you played to your maximum ability and if you made one or two particularly effective shots against your opponent, you can walk off the court feeling good about yourself and your foe. If you can come back and meet your opponent the next day or the next week for another game, you're that much farther ahead.

Choose Your Game

Choosing to play singles or doubles can also have an enormous impact of your enjoyment of tennis. Singles pits you against one other player and offers a truer test of your all-around abilities. You have to cover the entire court on your side of the net, which can involve considerable physical exertion. Doubles pairs you with a partner, which cuts down the amount of court area for which you're responsible and also distributes the burden of winning and losing between two people. You can play doubles effectively with less of a shot repertoire than you need for singles. In doubles, you can also enjoy a more tactical game, where strategies and ruses come into play more often.

Points to Ponder

In their 1983 book *The Tennis Grand Masters: How To Play Winning Tennis In The Prime Of Life*, authors Alvin W. Bunis and Roger Williams lay out five keys to success. They include:

1. Slow down and ease up.
2. Be steady and safe.
3. Don't underestimate the age gap.
4. Conserve energy.
5. Stay in shape.

Let's consider the wisdom of these recommendations. First, the power game of youth doesn't hold up well for senior players. If you bash the ball on every point and continually rush the net, you'll wear yourself down before the first set (game? point?) is over. Readjust your game to rely on efficiency rather than brute strength, on smooth strokes rather than vicious attacks, on lobs rather than overhead smashes.

Secondly, consistency counts more in senior tennis than placing tricky shots or making bold moves. Hit the ball so it clears the net with room to spare and keep your shots deep in your opponent's court. He will be less tempted to attack by rushing the net if he can sit back on the baseline and make an easy return of his own.

Third, although there is plenty of anecdotal evidence to the contrary, playing against men or women who are considerably younger than yourself can be frustrating. They can simply hit the ball harder and run around the court longer than you can. Unless they're willing to handicap you (which can be done), you're creating an uneven playing situation.

Fourth, use the time between points and sets to catch your breath. Let someone else retrieve the balls on the court if that's an option. If you're playing a friend, don't be embarrassed to take a bread and let your body recover. Your opponent will understand and may feel comfortable enough to ask for a break of his own later in the match.

And finally, conditioning your body requires steady and constant practice. You need to stretch before and after playing, and on the days that you don't play, too. You need to work your heart and lungs, both on and off the court. You need to watch your nutrition and food intake. Treat your body as the biomechanical machine that it is, providing it with proper fuel, lubrication and exercise.

DRILLS

Like any sport that requires hand-eye coordination, movement and strategy, tennis can be improved through practice. We've mentioned some drills throughout the text. Following are additional exercises which you may find both challenging and helpful for your game.

Watching the Seams of the Ball

You're probably heard the old adage to "keep your eyes on the ball," which is applied to everything from business to baseball. Tennis has its own variation on the theme. Scientists doubt whether you can actually see the ball hit your racket and bounce back because this event takes place in a fraction of a second. The discipline of focusing on the ball, however, is one worth pursuing even if it's ultimately unobtainable.

With its seams, its nappy fuzz, its brand name and its variety of colors, a tennis ball is actually a fairly intriguing visual object. By concentrating on the ball as it approaches, you can determine some important information, including how fast it's traveling and what kind of spin it has. The latter will determine, to some degree, which way it will bounce once it lands on the court or strikes your racket if you're hitting a volley.

A simple drill, then, is to focus on the ball while it's in flight. You can do this while rallying, while hitting against a wall or with a ball machine, or just by bouncing it into the air on your racket. Putting your attention on the ball will help take your mind off other factors, many of which don't need your conscious attention. For example, if you're observing the ball's spin, you won't be worrying about the score of the game or if you've got your racket pulled back to the right position. This zen-like attention to the ball can help aid your body's natural movement.

Mini-Tennis

Mini-tennis is both a good drill for learning to control your shots and for warming up. To play, both players stand at the service line and hit the ball so that it lands between the net and the service line on the other side. You can't hit the ball hard in this drill, so you have to contrate on placing the ball and warming up your body as you gently swing your racket. You can vary the game by hitting alternately forehand and back-hand shots, or by placing the ball on one side of the centerline and then the other. You can also hit the ball in the air so that you and your partner can practice making short volley strokes.

Groundstrokes

Groundstrokes are the bread and butter of tennis. When you trust your forehand and backhand, you can play with confidence and enjoy your game. There are many ways to practice these shots, including hitting with a ball machine, playing aginst a wall or rallying with a partner.

The key elements of a groundstroke are consistency, depth, placement and power. You can work on each of these separately or together by doing such drills as seeing how many times you can get the ball over the net in a row, how far back in your opponent's court you can place each shot, how well you can move the ball from one side of the court to the other and back again, and how hard you can hit the ball without losing consistency, depth and placement. While rallying, set goals for yourself, such as getting ten shots in a row within a foot of your partner's baseline, or picking a spot on the court and seeing how close you can get your shots to that point.

Volleying

The key to volleying is hitting the ball when it's out in front of you. Players who swing their rackets back for a volley often have problems with hitting the ball late, which reduces both control over the shot and the pace on the return. Unlike groundstrokes, where you have time to set up while the ball bounces and travels to the back of the court, volleys must be executed quickly.

One way to learn to meet the ball out in front on the volley is to stand with your back against a wall or a fence. Have your partner throw a ball towards you. The barrier behind you will eliminate your ability to take a backswing. At the same time that you bring the racket forward to meet the ball, step into the return. The transfer of weight forward will provide the power you need to make a solid return. As you become more comfortable with this motion, see if you can hit the ball directly back to your partner so that he can catch it with one hand. Practice this exercise on both the forehand and backhand sides.

Serving

No matter what level of tennis you play, your serve plays an important role. For beginners and intermediates, a reliable serve gets the ball into play and avoids the frustration of double faulting. For more advanced players, a strong or crafty serve (one with lots of spin) is a valuable weapon in match play.

Older players rely more on spin serves, where the racket is brushed across the ball in the serving motion to impart spin. These serves have several advantages over the flat serve, which is hit straight on and relies on raw power. You can hit a spin serve hard, like a flat serve, but the curve on the ball will tend to keep it in your opponent's service court. The spin will also make the ball jump into the air or to the side when it hits the court, which can throw your opponent's timing off and hopefully force him into a weak return. And if you're rushing the net, an effective spin serve gives you more time than a flat serve to get into position to volley your opponent's return.

One way to practice imparting spin on your serve is to stand six to eight feet away from the fence (which is usually ten feet high) that encloses the tennis court. The object is to reach up and over as you serve, imparting top spin on the ball so that it will clear the fence and then drop into the court. Another drill is to imagine that the net on the court is much higher, say the height of a volleyball net, than the regulation three feet. By putting top spin or side spin on the ball, you'll be able to clear this higher barrier and have the ball drop into your opponent's service court.

INSPIRATION

Who can say what allows some of us to enjoy physical activity well past the norm? Is it perhaps the physical activity itself? Researchers have found that *Los Viejos* (The Old Ones) of the Vilcabamba Valley in the Andes Mountains, home of the oldest living person in the Western Hemisphere, exercise vigorously every day in pursuit of their livelihoods as farmers. For those of us living in the mechanized, industrialized Western world, necessity does not force manual labor upon us. For the most part, using our bodies is our choice, and the evidence clearly indicates that those who make that choice live longer and more vigorous lives.

SUPER-SENIOR TENNIS

Given this premise, you may not be surprised to find that there are more than a few tennis players who are active well into their 80s and 90s. Many of the men in this category belong to Super-Senior Tennis, Inc., an national organization with a membership of about 3,000.

The birth of Super-Seniors Tennis dates back to 1963, when the first tournament for players 55 and older took place in Knoxville, Tennessee. Prior to that time, older men were only able to enter competitions that included much younger players. The organization soon took off, and included divisions for players in five year groups up to the age of 90. As current players approach the century mark, they will undoubtably push for even more divisions.

Writing in the January 1975 issue of *World Tennis* magazine, Eldon Roark, an avid Super-Senior player, wrote that "a person unfamiliar with the age restrictions (of Super-Senior Tennis) would never suspect that those agile, driving, smashing players are as old as they are. It is only when they remove their hats and caps and reveal their bald heads or gray hair that you get a clue to their ages. It doesn't show in their legs."

The individual stories of some of the Super-Senior Tennis players illustrate the possibilities of tennis as an important part of a long life:

Ken Beer

Born in 1903, Ken Beer of California started carrying a racket as a 30-year-old Pan Am pilot flying to Central American and the South Pacific. He found the game to be an excellent antidote to the fatigue that built up from flying noisy propellor planes for many hours at a stretch.

When he retired in 1963, he started playing tournaments and winning with regularity. Holder of dozens of national titles, he has reigned over his age group for more than a decade.

Beer feels that the importance of tennis is that the game offers him a challenge, without which he says people just don't thrive. He practices every day, hitting as many as 1,000 balls from a ball machine, an exercise that takes up the better part of two hours. Beer pursues what he calls a "relaxed training" regime, which means that he does what he wants and when he gets tired, he quits. "I don't overdue anything," he says, "but I do what I want. I play tennis every day. I run. I ski. I do a lot of gardening and I walk whenever I can." He credits his success to constant practice, focusing on hitting more accurately and with greater power. "I don't move as fast as I used to," he admits, "but I'm a lot faster than most other 90-year-olds!"

Malcolm Clarke

Beer's arch rival for the past ten years has been Malcolm Clarke of Maine, who is one year older than the Californian. Clarke played as a youth, winning the New England Boys title in 1917 and reached the semifinals in the national championships the same year. Tournament play took a back seat after graduation from college and during his career as a language teacher.

After retiring in 1962, he moved to a farm in

Maine, where cleaning out woods and gardening whipped him into good physical shape. He had pursued recreational tennis throughout his life, and at 75 he re-entered tournament play. Sixty years after his regional boys championship victory at the Longwood Cricket Club in Boston, he returned to the same venue and captured first place again! In 1992, the 90-year-old won three national tournaments and had his picture featured in *Sports Illustrated* magazine.

Clarke's advises those who want to learn the game to play as much as possible and against different partners in order to expand your game.

Although he divides his time between singles and doubles, he prefers the former as a conditioning exercise. He also good humoredly advises senior players to capitalize on guile. "I may swing at the ball hard these days," he says, "but it doesn't go over the net very fast. I like to use treachery whenever I can. For example, most players try to run their opponents by hitting the ball from side to side, but they're forgetting that the court also has depth. I might follow a deep shot with a drop shot just over the net to force the other player to run up and back and well as side to side. Use all the dimensions of the court."

Ferd Kramer

Born in 1901, Chicago's Ferd Kramer contends that "tennis is counter-aging. I'm sure I wouldn't still be here if it weren't for tennis." A recreational player since 1922, Kramer didn't start tournament play until 1975, three years after he had his first of four pacemakers installed to keep his pulse from dropping below 70 beats per minute. Kramer plays three times a week for two hours at a time and, like Clarke, has learned to rely less on power and more on a variety of shots, including lobs, drop shots and angled shots. Finding a partner his own age is the most frustrating part of his game, and he regularly plays against men and women who are 15 to 20 years younger. Both his cardiologist and his hemotologist urge him to continue playing as long as he can.

Herbert Hauser

Herbert Hauser has also received the blessing of his doctors to play. Five years younger than Kramer, Hauser had a narrowing of the aortic valve in the mid-1980s, a condition that led to some heart failure in 1988. Doctors implanted a pig's aortic valve as a replacement and within a couple of months, Hauser was back on the courts. His regular schedule includes playing four days a week, both singles and doubles, and usually against younger players. "I like to kid people and tell them I've got a 20-year guaranty on my heart!" he says.

Cleveland's city champion in 1923, Hauser took up tennis when he was 10 and played competitively through college. Among his fondest memories of high school was an exhibition in Cleveland given by the great Wimbledon champion Bill Tilden, an event that still influences his play 70 years later. "Tilden utilized the spin of the ball," he recalls, "and he made every shot a little differently. He told us that was the way to keep your opponent off balance. I still apply that principle to my own game."

York Jue

Standing no taller than 5 foot 3 inches tall and weighing no more than 123 pounds, California's 80-year-old York Jue (as in "New York Jew," he quips) can strike fear in players half his age and twice his size. His variety of shots, including strong and accurate ground strokes as well as a tennis bag full of chops, spins and slices, makes him one of the top rated players in the country.

A former accountant and auditor, Jue has spent 65 years refining his game. He follows an active training schedule, hitting balls from a ball machine on some days and against the wall at the local high school on other days. He finds the ball machine especially helpful in honing his drop shot, which he says is a valuable weapon against other seniors.

"I try not to let my opponents stand still," says Jue, whose two sons are active players as well. "I make them move from side to side, up and back and I like to change the pace of my return."

Jue has overcome several disabilities in pursuit of his favorite sport. In 1981, he had several feet of his colon removed and has worn a colostomy bag ever since. Six months after the operation, he fell backwards trying to hit an overhead and suffered a severe head injury. "You need to come back slowly after an injury," he says, although he admits it's sometimes hard to know when to slow down. Diehard senior players "need to get their rest," he adds.

"SUPER" WOMEN SENIORS

Women are not part of the Super Seniors tour, but they do have their own group which acts as a lobbying group for their interests. Many of the 1000 members of the National Senior Women's Tennis Association compete in the US Tennis Association regional and national tournaments.

As a group, women are not as strong as the men in the 80- and 90-year-old categories, due in part to their home-bound roles that many women of this age have lived with for the better part of the past century. There are exceptions, of course, and the imbalance will correct itself in coming years as women increasingly claim their rights to the pursuit of recreational sports. Here are some women who have already begun that transition:

Susan Tully
After a very successful junior and college ca-

reer in tennis, Susan Tully, 53, of Michigan took time off from the sport to raise her family. Two decades later, she resumed playing and entered the senior women's circuit, where she has again achieved high ranking.

As she ages, Susan finds that she approaches tennis more and more from the viewpoint of dance. She now focuses on efficiency of movement, footwork and balance, as well as emphasizing how to move to the ball. "I'm watching my opponent's movement and her racket preparation to judge the most likely angle of return," she says. "I've become more patient, waiting for the right angle to make a move."

Sue Anawalt

Sue Anawalt, 52, of California was Tully's doubles partner in college. She too took a sabbatical from the game after completing her education and returned ten years later to find her skills still intact.

"Your game slows down as you get older," she says. "A 50-year-old women just can't run as fast as she did before, but technically I've improved." She has a better understanding of the game and how to use the court. She's also learned how to use her body more efficiently, especially when serving the ball. "Women have tended to not use their legs well in the serve," she observes. "Good players bend their knees and rise up to meet the ball. It's not a strength issue, but one of timing."

Anawalt also religiously follows a stretching routine, supplementing her flexibility with yoga. "I'll never be as strong as I was at 20," she says, "but I still have a lot of capacity for strength and resiliency."

Elaine Mason

A veteran of 33 years of teaching elementary tennis at a California state university, Elaine Mason, 67, didn't actually play much tennis herself until the 1980s. After six years of recreational play, she began playing tournament matches as a way of challenging herself. "At first I wasn't 'tournament tough'," she says. "I had to learn to focus and not be tentative. Playing tournament matches has really helped my game."

Mason is credited with inventing a short racket to aid new players in learning the game. The truncated racket was part of her "graduated length method" of teaching. Mason had great success introducing her students to the mechanics of hitting the ball by starting first with the hand, then the short (22 to 24 inches long) racket and finally the full size (27 inch) version. This approach allows neophytes to develop the component skills of each of the four basic strokes — forehand, backhand, volley and overhead — by concentrating on body rotation, point of contact and transfer of weight. Short rackets are still available and, although marketed toward junior players, can be used by students of any age.

EQUIPMENT

QUITE A RACKET

Like the sport with which it is associated, the tennis racquet has deep historical roots. In his book *Tennis: Game of Motion,* author Eugene Scott says that the name itself has been traced back to Arabic, where the word *rahah*, meaning the palm of the hand, can be found. Medieval English contributes *rackle* and Latin has *rec*, both of which refer to a framework.

If you're over 50, you have probably either played tennis with a wooden racket or recall others doing so. For the better part of 600 years, wood was the material of choice, starting with the fourteenth century *battoir*, which was shaped like a canoe paddle. The rules governing racket shape and size have always been somewhat lax, with a resulting wide range of shapes and sizes, including triangles, circles and elliptical shaped heads. In his book *Tennis Your Way*, Nick Bollettieri notes that the first U.S. Open champion, Richard Sears, used a rectangularly shaped racquet.

Technological Advances

Originally molded from a single strip of wood, rackets underwent a major transformation in the 1920s when manufacturers began gluing strips of wood together to form stronger and more warp-resistant laminates. Advances in metal and plastic technology began to make inroads into wood's dominance 40 years later. In 1966, France's Rene LaCoste made a racket out of tubular steel, which soon became the rage. Over the next two decades the racket makers have also employed aluminum, fiberglass, graphite, boron, ceramics (a mixture of silicon, boron and aluminum in an epoxy matrix) and probably a few eyes of newt as well.

A Head of His Time

A few years after LaCoste's breakthrough, Howard Head, inventor of the first aluminum snow ski, turned his attention to tennis. Frustrated with his inability to improve his game through expensive lessons, he opted to change his equipment instead. Head came up with the idea for a bigger faced racket, one with 50 percent more hitting area than the conventional model. Head's patented oversize model provided an enlarged "sweet spot" with which to contact the ball. The larger hitting surface also twisted less when the ball hit off center and sent fewer potentially damaging vibrations up the player's arm.

The advantages offered by Head's racket prompted other manufacturers to follow suit as much as they could — Head's patent covered rackets with a hitting area between 85 and 130 square inches — and they turned out mid-size models just under the 85-square-inch limit. The old standard rackets with 79 square inches or less of hitting surface are now almost as obsolete as the wooden frame.

Moving to a Wide Body

Most recently, racket frames have grown in width as well. In 1984, engineer/author Siegfried Kuebler of Germany wrote a novel about a tennis coach who invented a special racket that moved back with the impact of the ball and returned each shot more efficiently and accurately. Out of this fantasy came Kuebler's idea for a so-called "wide body" frame, which has more thickness than traditional frames. The designer's prototype proved very successful, offering great striking power, low vibration and a solid feel.

You can fit your racket to your style of play. Use a flexible racket if you like to stay at the baseline and hit long shots or choose a stiffer model if you like to rush the net and punch short shots with little backswing. For the senior player, larger and more powerful rackets have spiced up the game, giving back through technology some of the elements, such as consistency and pace, that the years may have taken away.

CHOOSING A RACKET

In this era of multiple consumer choices, you can find a racket to meet just about any budget and any level of playing skill. Rather than making your selection easier, this overwhelming array of choices may make things more difficult. That's the reality of modern sports marketing, however. Here are some guidelines that might aid you in navigating the tennis racket maze.

Price

You can get a reasonably good racket at a sporting goods store or through a mail order company for $30 to $60. For the more advanced or style-conscious player, rackets can be purchased for $200 or more. At a certain price, however, the racket in your hand will be no better than the mind and body of the player attached to it.

Size

The larger the hitting surface of the racket, the larger will be the sweet spot, or the area on the strings that deliver a smooth, powerful and controlled shot. Traditional racket heads had a hitting surface ranging from 60 to 79 square inches, but they have given way in popularity to midsize and oversize rackets in recent years. Midsize frames present 80 to 95 square inches of hitting surface, while oversize frames range from 96 to

115 square inches. There are even super-oversize models for those who want to maximize their chances of getting the racket on the ball. Most players these days are using the midsize and oversize models.

Wide body rackets have also become popular since their introduction in the mid-1980s. Thicker in cross-section than traditional rackets, the wide bodies add as much as 15 percent extra stiffness to the racket frame. From the beginner to the expert, this technological breakthrough automatically adds more power to players' ground strokes. Like midsize and oversize rackets, wide bodies are easy to find at your sporting goods retailer and through mail order outlets.

Materials

Wood has given way to a wide array of space age materials used in the construction of modern rackets. All of these materials, which include graphite, ceramic composites and Kevlar, are light and durable. Some emphasize strength and others are especially stiff. How these materials are arranged in the racket — how they are used to take advantage of their unique properties — determines the quality of the final product.

Test Drive Your Racket

Since your racket becomes an extension of yourself on the court, it's a good idea to spend some time making your choice. One good place to start is a shop that specializes in tennis equipment where you're more than likely to find someone who can match your needs with the appropriate racket.

Getting a Grip

If you're a beginner, you want a racket that fits your hand and feels comfortable when you hold and swing it. The salesperson can help you size your hand for the appropriate grip, or you can do it yourself. There are several methods for this measurement, some of which are more arcane than others. Perhaps the best rule of thumb, literally, is to grasp the racket handle so that the strings are aligned vertically. Close your fingers around the handle and notice where the tip of your thumb is relative to the first joint of your middle finger. If the two are touching or slightly overlapping, you're in the ballpark.

Questions to Ask

If you're a more advanced player, bring your old racket to the store when you're shopping for a new one. A salesperson can use the old model as a starting point in your discussions, during which you should find answers to several questions. Among them are:

- How frequently do you play?
- Are you an aggressive, tournament competitor or a recreational/social player?

- Do you like to rush the net or do you prefer to hit from the baseline?
- Do you have any special wrist/elbow/shoulder problems that need to be taken into consideration?
- How much do you want to spend?

Rent a Racket, or Two or Three

Tennis retailers will often let you rent rackets to give them a test drive, and the fee they charge for this service may be applied towards a purchase at their store. Depending on your seriousness, you may want to rent out a couple or more models. Try them out against one of your regular partners so he or she can tell you if the racket makes any difference in your hitting. Run the test models through the gamut of shots and see how it feels. This is another way to test the proper handle size, as well. If the racket twists in your hand when you contact the ball, or if your hand and arm tire quickly, the grip may be the wrong size.

String and Tensions

You can buy new rackets either strung or unstrung. In the case of the former, you play with what the manufacturer felt was best for that particular model. For most beginners and recreational players, this solution obviates the need to get into decisions about type and tension of strings. As you become more proficient at the game, however, the subtleties of string thickness and string tension will become more important.

String Guidelines

General guidelines to remember about strings include the following:

- Thinner strings tend to be more elastic and enhance your ability to impart spin on the ball. Thicker strings will last longer, but have less ability to grab or cup the ball on impact.

- The days of gut string are essentially over. A few players still use gut, which is made from beef intestine. The overwhelming majority now play with nylon strings, which are more durable and resist the effects of moisture.

- Strings lose tension whether you play with them or not. Depending on what kind of surface you play on and what kind of game you play, strings will wear out at different rates. Grit from clay courts will abrade strings. Slower surfaces, such as clay and grass, tend to keep the ball in play longer, so you take more hits per point. The stiffer wide body rackets tend to put more pressure on strings, which may wear them out more rapidly. The general guideline for restringing is to have it done per year as many times as you play per week. If, therefore, you play twice a week, have your racket restrung twice a year.

- Contrary to what you might think, a more loosely strung racket generates more power than a tightly strung one. The latter, however, offers more control. The exact reasons for this still escape conclusive scientific research. The general theory is that looser strings deflect more when the ball strikes the racket and trampoline the ball back with greater force. Conversely, the ball tends to flatten when it strikes tightly strung rackets and the strings "grab" the ball better. For those with tender elbows, looser strings offer more give and should be factored into the equation.

- String tension also varies with the size of your racket head. In general, larger head rackets require more tension than smaller head versions. Probably the best course for beginners and recreational players is to go with the manufacturer's recommended guidelines for your racket. Experience will lead you to experiment with string tensions when you reach a higher level of play.

- If you've ever watched professional or even good tournament players, you'll notice that they will, between points, adjust the strings of their racket. When the ball strikes the strings, they are sometimes deflected from their normal rectangular configuration. By pushing the strings back into position, you are recreating a uniform pattern and ensuring a more predictable ball response. You're also helping prevent undue stress on any one string, a move that should help prevent breakage. There are also plastic tabs which can be inserted at the string intersections to help prevent string movement.

- Strings do break, and often there can be no warning signals. One way to ensure that you will still be able to play if you do have a mishap is to bring an extra racket.

TENNIS BALLS

Like rackets, tennis balls come in many varieties. Some of the factors that differentiate balls are the amount of wool nap covering the rubber surface, the amount of pressure (or lack of it) and color. White balls, which used to be the norm, are now oddities. Yellow, orange or a combination of the two are most popular these days.

Heavy-Duty and Championship Balls

Balls with heavy wool nap are called, appropriately, heavy or extra duty balls, and are designed for use on hard courts. On soft courts like clay, these balls will sometimes fluff up and become heavy. Balls designated as "championship" quality have less nap and can be used on softer courts without the fluffing problem. The cham-

however, and tend to wear out sooner.

Pressurized Balls

Pressurized balls are packed in vacuum-sealed containers before leaving the manufacturer's factory. This accounts for the rush of air that you hear when you pop the top off a can. New balls are relatively bouncy, a characteristic they will hold for a while depending on how often you use them, but generally not longer than a week's time. After that, they can be kept for use as practice balls or passed on to the dog and/or kids.

Non-Pressurized Balls

Non-pressurized balls circumvent the issue of losing pressure and therefore have a longer playing life. They also tend to be heavy and lack the zip of the pressurized version.

Non-pressurized balls can also be used at any altitude without significant performance differences. The same cannot be said for pressurized balls, whose performance varies considerably whether you're playing at sea level or in the mountains. A sea level ball, for example, will act more like a child's super bouncy rubber ball when used at a high altitude site.

TENNIS SHOES

Like rackets, tennis shoe styles and models have increased exponentially over the past decade. Athletic shoe technology in general has become increasingly sophisticated, with commensurate pricing increases. Gone are the days of strapping on your Keds or your Stan Smiths and hitting the court.

Factors to Consider

Finding the right pair of shoes for yourself can be a challenge. There are several factors to consider, including:

• The Type of Surface You Play On

Different types of material used in the sole of the shoe are better suited for different types of surfaces. On a clay court, for example, you expect to slide on the grainy surface. On a hard court, you stop and start suddenly. A shoe designed for one type of playing surface probably won't perform well on the other.

• Your Style of Play

If you hit mostly from the baseline, your most frequently repeated movements are from side to side. If you rush the net, you're moving ahead and back much of the time. Each movement demands something different of your footwear. You may also be someone who drags his toe, either on serves or even on groundstrokes. This habit can wear out the toe cap before the rest of the shoe.

- **Your History and Preference for Athletic Shoes**

If you grew up playing either tennis or other sports in low cut sneakers, you may feel uncomfortable wearing ¾ or high cuts, which rise to the ankle bones. The opposite is also true. You may also have a strong nostalgic attachment to a particular brand of shoe and want to continue playing with that manufacturer's latest model.

- **Your Foot Structure**

People's feet are as individualized as their hands. Toes, ankles and arches all bear the imprints of geneology, socialization and health habits. The new generation of sneakers take some of these variations into account. If your foot supinates, or rolls excessively to the outside, you need a shoe with added lateral support and cushioning. If you foot pronates, or rolls excessively to the inside, you need extra support on the inside portion.

Buying New Shoes

Here are some suggestions to keep in mind when you make the trip to the store to buy your next pair of tennis shoes:

- Take your old pair of sneakers with you. Based on the wear patterns of your used shoes, a qualified shoe salesperson can spot areas where you need extra support and cushioning.

- Try on both pairs of shoes. One of your feet may be bigger than the other. You may also find that as you age, your foot size may change. Wear the same number of socks that you play in when you try on the shoes. Also, the time of day may affect your size. Feet tend to swell late in the day.

- Make sure they fit. Unlike leather dress shoes which get broken in with wearing, athletic shoes are pretty much a what-you-feel-is-what-you-get proposition. Your heel should fit snugly in the cup at the back of the shoe. Your toes should have room to move freely without swimming in the toe box or being pinched. Your midfoot region should be held firmly.

- Find out if they're suitable for the court you usually play on. A herringbone pattern on the sole of the shoe is considered better for clay surfaces because it allows your foot to slide and doesn't pick up the clay material. Hard court players will find more success with open geometric shapes, also called pillars, on the bottom of their shoes. Likewise, synthetic polyurethane soles grab less than rubber soles, making the former better for hard courts and the latter preferable for clay and soft courts.

COMMON TENNIS PROBLEMS AND HOW TO DEAL WITH AND/OR AVOID THEM

Anyone who plays the game of tennis at a recreational or higher level has to be concerned with injuries. At some point or other, no matter how much you warm up and stretch, there will be an overhead smash or a wide shot off the court that will cause you to put yourself in a position where your body will be at risk.

Injuries are nothing to be ashamed of, nor are they to be ignored. "Playing through the pain" is another well worn and generally disproved myth. The best thing you can do when you sustain an injury is stop playing and take measures to heal yourself, which may mean taking a day or two off, or seeing a doctor for medical care.

AVOIDANCE IS THE BEST (PREVENTATIVE) MEDICINE

The best way to deal with injuries, of course, is to avoid them. Proper technique and equipment, adequate physical conditioning and maintaining awareness of your surroundings at all times are all factors that go into the prevention of injury.

THE *RICE* TREATMENT

If you do sustain an injury to muscle, bone or joint, proper and immediate attention are crucial. In fact, the first day and a half after an injury is the time to concentrate on limiting the swelling and inflammation that result from the mishap. Standard practice for athletic injuries includes adherence to four basic actions which go by the acronym *RICE*. They are:

- *R* for rest and reducing the use of the injured body part until the pain and swelling go away. You can exercise other parts of your body, as long as the activity doesn't aggravate the injury.

- *I* for ice, which is applied to the injured area to reduce swelling, bleeding, inflammation and pain. The cold constricts the blood vessels, which prevents fluid from rushing in and causing swelling. Ice chips in a plastic bag, ice frozen in a paper cup or even frozen vegetables (such as peas) in a plastic bag can all be used for this purpose. Put a layer of cloth, such as a sock or towel, between the ice and the skin to prevent injury to the skin from the cold. Ice for 20 minutes as soon as possible after the injury occurs, and repeat the process several times over the next few days. Do not use heat during the first day and half, as this may cause swelling. Once the acute pain of the injury has subsided, which should take two or three days, heat can be used to help relax the muscles and promote healing.

- *C* for compressing the injury to further prevent swelling. An elastic bandage wrapped firmly, but not too tightly, around the painful area will do the trick. You can combine icing and compression at the same time, placing the ice pack inside the elastic bandage.

- *E* for elevation. Resting the injured area above the level of your heart allows gravity to help reduce the swelling by draining excess fluid.

HEALING AGENTS

Painkillers are a subject about which you need to consult with your doctor. Anti-inflammatory drugs, such as aspirin, can be a great benefit when you suffer a muscular or skeletal injury, provided they are used properly and not as a way to mask the pain from an injury while you continue to aggravate it. Equally as potent as drugs are patience and time, both of which allow the body to mend itself as it was designed to do.

TENNIS ELBOW

Given the mechanics of tennis, where you are essentially lengthening your arm by means of a racket and attempting to hit a semi-solid object (an air-inflated tennis ball), unnatural strains and stresses are going to occur. The most common point at which these strains tend to accumulate is the elbow, and the resulting injuries have earned the generic moniker "tennis elbow." Members of the general population suffer from this discomfort at a rate of about two persons per hundred. Among tennis players, however, the number shoots up to one in three. While the condition afflicts weekend and recreational players for the most part, even professionals are not immune from its pain. Those who play more frequently, such as four or more times a week, are more prone to tennis elbow as well.

What Is Tennis Elbow?

Medically, tennis elbow is often referred to as tendonitis, or an inflammation of the tendons that attach to the lower portion of the upper arm. These tendons run over the bulbous stump of the humerus bone. This structure is resilient enough to handle the normal overloads that occur during training and exercise. If the bones and muscles undergo repetitive and/or sudden stress, however, the normal restorative process breaks down.

Studies have shown that the forces converging on these tendons are indeed severe. Racket speed just prior to contact with the ball on a serve, for example, can reach over 300 mph for an advanced player. Contact with the ball cuts that velocity in half within a matter of milliseconds. The impact of that deceleration is absorbed by the forearm muscles and their tendons at the humerus. The convergence of these mechanical forces can stretch the tendons beyond their usual limit. The result is small tears at the muscles' roots. The tissues which replace the tears tend to be not as efficient as the originals. They heal slowly and cause pain.

Symptoms

The primary symptom of tennis elbow is pain at the joint that is not associated with any accident or known injury. You may feel a dull ache that radiates down the forearm. The pain can be reproduced by shaking hands or by extending the middle finger against resistance. If not treated and corrected, tennis elbow can become chronic, reducing your grip strength and possibly leading to the formation of calcium deposits in the elbow.

THE TWO TYPES OF TENNIS ELBOW
Medial Tennis Elbow

There are two types of tennis elbow. Pain on the inside portion, near the "funny bone," is called medial tennis elbow, and is usually produced by the serve or forehand stroke. One common cause for this type of problem is the result of hitting with a straight arm. In this position, your bicep muscle, which is the main stabilizing muscle of the arm, is fully extended and not capable of absorbing much shock. As a result, the elbow takes the load. By bending your arm, you allow the force of the impact to travel up the arm to the more substantial shoulder joint.

Creating Topspin Properly

Another contributor to medial tennis elbow is the tendency for players to roll the wrist and elbow in an attempt to put topspin on the ball. Unfortunately, the ball remains on the racket strings for such a short time that this movement has no effect on its spin.

Topspin is generated by the path of the racket, from low to high, as you bring it through the ball. The face of the racket should be perpendicular when it contacts the ball. The upward path of the racket head will brush the strings across the ball and automatically impart topspin.

Loosen Up On Overhead Shots

On the serve and overhead shots, which include a forward snapping of the wrist just after you hit the ball, loosening your grip may help. One technique which helps you ease up on your grip is to hold the racket with just the thumb and forefinger as you serve. This will take the last three fingers, the ones that control the tendons which tighten the wrist, out of the picture. You won't have as much control over the racket using this grip, which means you'll have to slow down your stroke to keep from losing the racket altogether and to keep your shot on target.

Lateral Tennis Elbow

Pain on the outside section of the arm, called lateral tennis elbow, results from problems associated with the backhand stroke. The lateral version tends to be more common, especially among recreational players who don't develop the proper mechanics for the stroke. How to hit a proper backhand is a discussion that has been written about many times. There appears to be general agreement that the main culprit in a poor backhand — one that often results in tennis elbow — is the tendency to lead with your elbow.

Keep Your Elbow Down

Biomechanical research shows that players with less risk of tennis elbow drop their leading shoulder as they prepare to hit and cock their racket arm so that the tip of the elbow is pointing toward the ground. The power of the shot comes from rotating the upper body with the racket arm acting simply as an extension of the that movement.

Those who suffer from tennis elbow tend to rely more on their arm alone to make the shot. These players raise their leading shoulder and bend the elbow slightly as they prepare to hit. The tip of the elbow is pointing at the net. The power in this case comes from pulling the upper arm across the body, which is a much weaker and less efficient technique. This type of hitting places even more severe stress on the elbow, since you have the force of the ball's impact on the racket pulling one way on the elbow and the muscles of the upper arm pulling in the opposite direction.

Extend Your Racket Arm

Another indicator of poor backhand technique is using the thumb on the backhand side of the racket to help push the ball over the net. This technique reinforces the habit of making the elbow the center of rotation, a purpose for which the joint was not designed. The racket arm should be extended, but not rigid, which makes the ball and socket joint of the shoulder a more appropriate center of rotation.

Identifying Poor Technique

Other factors that might force a player to use poor technique in the backhand include inadequate preparation, too small a grip, a lack of strength in gripping the racket or a lack of arm strength in general. All of these can be remedied or improved upon. You can, for example, set up properly for the shot by getting yourself positioned so that you swing freely and easily, and not be jammed by the ball like a baseball player trying to hit an inside pitch off the wrists.

Doctors say they see more tennis elbow in men, a phenomenon that suggests that the condition afflicts those trying to swing too hard, as men are apt to do.One way to correct this habit is to slow your strokes down. Instead of using your arm to generate all the force, rely on the rotation of your torso and to transfer of weight as you step into the ball.

TREATING TENNIS ELBOW

Treatment of tennis elbow depends on the severity of the inflammation and pain. Obviously, you want to give the tendons a chance to heal. You can stop playing tennis, but that won't prevent you from using your hand for other gripping functions, like opening a door or driving a car. (Tennis elbow occurs in non-tennis players, especially carpenters, who use their hands to grip tools.)

Hot and Cold Treatment

For immediate treatment, ice and friction massage are recommended. The cold constricts the surface blood vessels and the friction dilates them. Alternating back and forth between the two promotes circulation, which, in theory, removes waste products from the surrounding tissue and imports new cells with fresh materials to heal the torn tissues.

Use ice to massage the sore area for three or four minutes. At first the elbow will feel cold, followed by burning, achiness and then numbness. When the last stage is reached, remove the ice and rub the area with the pad of your thumb or index finger. Start with a light touch and gradually increase the pressure. After another four minutes or so, the feeling will return to the elbow. Repeat the procedure again until you've worked on the area for a total of 15 to 20 minutes. Be sure to end each session with ice so as not to leave the area inflamed. This cold/hot massage should be repeated two or three times a day.

Rehabilitation for Tennis Elbow

Rest is an important part of the healing process, but some doctors like to take an aggressive approach with tennis elbow. Once the pain has subsided for a few days, you can start a stretching and strengthening program to help get your elbow and forearm back in shape to play again. After each of these sessions you should also apply ice for 20 minutes to prevent inflammation.

The forearm stretch, one of the U.S. Tennis Association's Basic 10 Flexibility Exercises (see Chapter 7), is a good stretch to help your recovery.

Strengthening Exercises

To strengthen the muscles of the forearm, place your arm on a desk or other surface so the upper arm and forearm form a 90° angle and your wrist extends over the edge by three or four inches. Use a light hand weight or a length of surgical tubing to perform wrist curls (with the palm facing upwards) and reverse wrist curls (with the palm facing down). Use a weight or resistance that permits you to do 20 to 30 repetitions. Do two sets of each exercise.

With your arm in the same position and your palm facing up, put your weight in your hand and slowly rotate it 180° so your palm ends up in the face down position. Then return it to the original position. Repeat this cycle 20 to 30 times.

You can also squeeze putty or a tennis ball to strengthen your grip, doing about 20 repetitions each session. Be careful not to overstrain the muscles that you're trying to heal.

Isometric Strengthening

There are other ways you can maintain the tone and even strengthen the forearm muscles used in tennis without actually playing. One way to do this is by isometric exercises with the racket. Leave the cover on your racket and find a doorjamb or a solid pole. Position yourself as if you were hitting a shot. Place the face of the racket against solid resistance at the point in your stroke where you make contact with the ball and press. Hold the pose for a count of 15 and release. Repeat again several times over the course of the day. You can do this exercise for the forehand, backhand and overhead/serve.

Surgery Is a Last Resort

The good news about tennis elbow is that surgery is used as a last resort and this remedy is rare. By following doctor's orders and adhering to a recuperation and rehabilitation program, tennis elbow sufferers can regain pain-free use of their arms once again. Recurrence of the malady can also be avoided by following the stretching and warming up guidelines we've already mentioned.

The Tennis Elbow Strap

Ever since Major Wingfield introduced the sport of lawn tennis in the late 1800s, tennis elbow has been known to physicians. An English surgeon described the symptoms back in 1882. The remedy at the time was restricted movement and the use of an elastic bandage or webbing around the elbow for support. In modern times, this bandage takes the form of an elbow strap. Cinched around the forearm just below the elbow, the device helps relieve the pain of tennis elbow. It should not, however, be considered a cure for the problem. The strap should be used in conjunction with other rehabilitative practices, including icing and stretching, warming up and using proper stroking technique.

How the Elbow Strap Works

While not all medical researchers agree on why the strap works, the general theory is that the device effectively shortens the length of the forearm muscles by pressing them together and into the bones of the forearm. The strain that results from hitting the ball is thus short-circuited from reaching the origins of the muscles where they attach to the humerus. The strap is most effective in dealing with pain from lateral tennis elbow. It may be counterproductive for those with medial tennis elbow, so before you buy one you might want to try it out to see if it solves your problem.

SHOULDER PROBLEMS

Next to the elbow, perhaps the joint called upon to do the most work in tennis is the shoulder. While larger and surrounded by more muscle, the shoulder is nevertheless susceptible to injury, due in part to the shallow socket in which the humerus rests. According to physical therapist Todd Ellenbecker, a group of four small muscles and tendons, called the rotator cuff muscles, hold the joint in place. These muscles start on the shoulder blade and attach to the top of the humerus.

The rotator cuff muscles are relatively weak in

comparison to the muscles that surround them. They can also be pinched between the bones in the shoulder when you raise your arms overhead as you would in serving the ball or hitting an overhead shot.

Deceleration in the Shoulder

Biomechanical research has shown that the rotator cuff muscles are also important in slowing the arm down in the follow-through after making a throwing motion. Examples would be pitching a baseball or hitting a serve. The deceleration following release of the ball, as in the case of a thrown pitch, or contact with the ball, as in the case of a tennis serve, is quite rapid and puts considerable stress on the shoulder muscles.

Strengthening the Rotator Cuff Muscles

Two simple exercises are recommended to help condition and strengthen the rotator cuff group. Do them with light weights in your hand, between one and five pounds. Use a weight that allows you to make ten repetitions of the movement without pain. Each exercise should be done in three sets of ten repetitions each and should be done on both sides for balance.

Start the first exercise by lying on your left side. Rest your right arm at your side and bend it 90° at the elbow. Simply raise your right hand as far as you can while keeping your elbow fixed at your side. Hold your arm in the raised position for two seconds and lower the weight back to the starting position.

The second exercise is done while standing with your arms hanging at your sides. To find the right position, imagine that straight ahead is 12 o'clock, 90° to the right is 3 o'clock and 90° to the left is 9 o'clock. Raise your right hand to shoulder level at the 3 o'clock position and then rotate it forward to the 2 o'clock position. Imagine that instead of a weight you're holding a can of water and you turn it upside down to spill the water on the ground. In this position, your thumb will be pointing straight down. Keep that position and lower your hand down to your side and back up to shoulder height. Repeat the movement on both sides.

DEALING WITH AN ACHING BACK

Since eight out of ten Americans suffer from back pain at one time or other in their lives, chances are you've had to deal with this ailment. Few aches or pains are as vexing and nettlesome as the ones that radiate from your lower back. For an athlete, even a weekend warrior, this type of pain can cause worry as well as discomfort. Not infrequently, back pain sufferers will ignore or deny the warning signals that something is wrong, hoping to "play through the pain." Unfortunately, this course can be even more damaging.

The prevalence of back pain in our society leads us to a good news/bad news scenario. The good news is that back pain has been studied in depth and a multitude of remedies are available. The bad news is that the root causes of the pain are still sometimes difficult to pin down, and not all of the cures available bring guaranteed relief.

Be Prudent

If you do suffer from back pain, don't continue exercising and hope that it will go away. Chances are it won't. Consult your doctor, who may refer you to an orthopedic specialist. The chances are good that your discomfort is being caused by muscular problems, such as lack of exercise, weak muscles or overweight. In such a case, training in proper back mechanics and specialized exercises to help relax and condition the muscles of both your back and your abdomen may yield positive results.

Be Gentle

You can take solace in the data showing that back pain usually clears up on its own accord with the passage of time. The length of time is greater than the soreness we associate with other muscles in the body, like a bruised thigh, however. Inactivity, while it might be recommended in some cases, is usually counterproductive in the treatment of lower back pain. Those of you who have suffered this type of pain know that sitting still can be one of the most uncomfortable positions of all!

Sore backs usually respond well to gentle movements. Daily walks of 20 to 30 minutes are great for warming and loosening the muscles of your lower back. As the tendons and muscles heal, you can slowly work your way back into more vigorous exercise. You may not be able to play a full set of tennis right away, but you can start by gently swinging the racket and hitting easily against the wall or with a partner and stopping before the pain flares up again.

Aids for Back Pain Sufferers

Other aids in playing tennis when you have experienced or are prone to back pain include:

- Playing on softer surfaces. If you have a choice between asphalt and a softer surface, such as clay, grass or a composite surface, choose one of the latter. If you can only play on a hard court, wear an extra pair of socks and tennis shoes with lots of cushion to absorb the shock.

- Paying attention to your back during play. Tennis involves vigorous torsion, flexion and extension movements, all of which can aggravate a bad back. Try to minimize those types of movements. For example, simplify your serve so that you don't arch your back excessively when you throw the ball overhead and hit it with your racket. Also, when you hit a forehand or backhand stroke, concentrate on moving your torso as a single unit to minimize the torsion on your back. You may also find relief in wearing a back brace, which will help keep your lower back from bending too far in any direction.

Increasing Your Flexibility

If you want to play tennis regularly, you need to work at increasing your flexibiity and suppleness so that back pain doesn't come back to haunt you on an ongoing basis. Here are some simple exercises you can do at home to help keep your back in shape:

• Pelvic Tilts

Lie on your back with your legs drawn up so that the soles of your feet rest flat on the floor. Notice that there's space between your lower back and the floor. Tilt your pelvis to make that space disappear. You do this by contracting your abdominal muscles. Hold that position for a count of five and release. Repeat the movement several times.

• Single Leg Pulls

In the same position as for the pelvic tilts, bring one knee up towards your chest and grasp it with your hands. Gently pull it closer to your chest and hold for a count of five. Keep breathing while you do this. Release the knee and let the leg return to its original position. Do the same movement with the other leg. Repeat the cycle several times. This motion will automatically lengthen your lower back (as the pelvic tilt did), as well as increasing flexibility in your hips and buttocks.

• Crunches

As mentioned earlier, one of the keys to controlling back pain is conditioning the abdominal muscles. The muscles in front of the body help maintain the natural curves in your spine. When your abdominal muscles are weak, they allow your intestinal wall to spill out over your pubic bone, which tips the pelvis forward and exaggerates the curve of your lower back. When the abdominal muscles are healthy and toned, they hold the intestinal wall straight up and down and relieve the pressure on the lower back.

Crunches are also performed while lying on your back with your legs drawn up so that the soles of your feet are on the floor. Your arms can be either at your side, crossed on your chest or with fingers laced behind your head and elbows spread out to the side. Raise your head slowly off the ground, keeping your gaze towards the ceiling. Don't jerk your head off the ground or try to raise your entire upper body off the floor. The raising of your head (and your arms if they're on your chest or behind your head) will cause the abdominal muscles to contract without putting too much stress on your lower back. Hold the position for a count of five and lower your head to the floor. Repeat the movement five times at first and build the number of repetitions as your abdomen gets stronger. The straight-ahead crunch will help tone the muscles in the center of your abdomen. To work on the lateral abdominal muscles, vary your crunch by turning slightly as you rise up. Turn to the right so that you're looking over your right knee, return to the floor and then turn to the left so that you're looking over your left knee as you rise up. Again, repeat each exercise five times and build the number of repetitions as you gain strength.

• The Swim

Lie on your stomach with your hands extended over your head. Let your forehead rest on the floor. Raise your right arm and left leg a few inches off the ground and then bring them back to rest. Do the same movement with your left arm and right leg. Repeat this five times at first and increase it as your back becomes stronger. This movement will condition the muscles that run up and down your spine.

• Cat Stretch

Using a padded mat or a rug, assume a position on all fours with your knees and hands spread shoulder-width apart. Start with your spine in a straight and relaxed position. Slowly breathe out and contract your abdomen and buttock muscles so that your back bows up into the air. Your head will naturally drop in response. Hold for a count of five. Inhale and release the contraction back to the starting position. To further stretch your back in this position, shift your weight backwards so that your legs fold up and your arms are extended out in front of you. Be careful of your knees in this position! Let your head rest on the floor. Hold this stretch for a count of five and then return to the starting position on all fours. Repeat this cycle several times.

KNEES

Traveling down the torso, we come next to another common problem area for tennis players and other athletes. In fact, next to the elbow and shoulder, the knees are probably the joints under the most stress during a tennis game. Medical research shows that one out of four sports injuries of all kinds involves the knees.

The largest joint in the body, the knee is also one of the most complex and most mobile. Running, bending and turning, which are all key elements to playing tennis, rely heavily on the proper functioning of the knee.

Avoiding Knee Problems

Self-diagnosing a knee injury is probably a useless pursuit unless you have extensive medical training or you've suffered the same injury before and know how it feels. You can help reduce the chances of suffering a knee injury by following some simple guidelines:

Pace Yourself

If you're playing tennis once a week for a couple of hours and then try to up that frequency to four or five times a week, you'll be placing your knees (and the rest of your body) under considerable stress. If you go to a week-long tennis camp, for example, you need to make sure you don't overload your knees and create an injury.

Wear Supportive Footwear

If your sneakers or tennis shoes are ill-fitting or worn down beyond their useful life, the stresses and strains which result as you stop and start on the court will be transferred up to the knee. If you have foot problems unrelated to the condition of your shoes, you may need to have special orthotic devices put in your shoes to correct lower leg alignment problems.

Keep Your Muscles in Good Condition

The quadriceps and the hamstring muscles on the front and back respectively of the thigh provide the power to the movements of the knee. They need to be stretched before and after playing tennis and exercised both on and off the court. Other types of exercise that work the thigh muscles are running and bicycling, to name just two.

Strengthening exercises for the thighs include:

- *half squats*. Stand with your feet shoulder-width apart and your toes pointed straight forward. Slowly bend your knees while keeping your back straight and vertical, and keep your knees over toes as you go down. You can hold onto a table or a wall for stability. Continue dropping your body until just before you have to either tilt your pelvis back or raise your heels to go any lower. Your thigh muscles should feel tension in this position. Hold the position for a count of five and then slowly raise yourself back to standing. Repeat the movement a few times at first, and build the number of repetitions as you gain strength in your thighs. Remember to breathe during the exercise!

- *knee extensions.* Sit on a desk or a counter-top with your lower legs hanging vertically over the edge. Hold onto the edge of the sitting surface with your hands. Slowly extend one leg at a time until the knee is fully extended. Hold that position for five counts and then slowly lower your leg to the original position. Again, repeat the movement a few times at first and build the number of repetitions as you gain strength. Then do the other leg. For more of a challenge, you can add a light weight (one to three pounds) to your ankles for added resistance.

- *straight leg lifts.* Lie on your back with one knee bent so that the sole of your foot rests on the floor. Protect your back by contracting your abdominal muscles and tilting your pelvis, which will eliminate the space between the floor and your lower back. Raise the straight leg no more than six to twelve inches off the floor and hold it for five seconds. Lower the straight leg slowly back to the floor. Repeat a few times and build the number of repetitions as you gain strength. You can also add a light weight to your ankles. If this exercise causes pain in your back, don't do it.

TENNIS LEG

Seen primarily in middle-aged tennis players, tennis leg refers to a strain in the gastrocnemius or calf muscle. The injury usually occurs when you forcefully push or lunge off one leg in an attempt to reach a wide shot. Women tend to have the problem more than men, which may have something to do with their history of wearing high heeled shoes. Often, the injury will be preceded by general fatigue, such as playing three sets of tennis in a row. Well conditioned athletes who tire less easily are less susceptible to tennis leg.

Tennis leg is characterized by pain on the inside part of the calf, an indicator that the muscle tissue has been torn. Muscle spasm usually follows the initial pain, and you will have trouble putting your heel down on the ground or bearing weight on the injured leg. You may have to be assisted from the court.

Aggressive Treatment

Immediate treatment and aggressive rehabilitation are recommended for tennis leg. The leg should be immediately iced and compressed to prevent inflammation and the pooling of blood in the lower leg. The two or three days following the injury will be painful until the internal bleeding stops. The calf muscle may also go into spasm when you sit or stand still, making it difficult to walk.

Don't Wait for Rehabilitation

Rehabilitation can and should start within a

couple of days of the injury. Your doctor will recommend drugs or electrical muscle stimulation if they are needed. A physical therapist can give you stretching and strengthening exercises which you can continue at home. A good stretch to deal with the pain of tennis leg, and to help prevent it in the first place, is the calf stretch. (See the *USTA Basic 10 Flexibility Exercises*, Chapter 7.)

Strengthening Exercises

There are a couple of strengthening exercises to help your calf muscle regain its tone. These can also be done after the injury has healed to keep the muscles in condition for further tennis play.

- Sit on the floor with your legs extended out in front of you. Take an elastic cord and loop it around the ball of your foot. Work with one foot at a time. Pull the elastic towards you and resist the pressure with your foot. Repeat the movement ten times; then rest and complete two more cycles of ten. Repeat the whole series three times a day.

- Heel raises are the other strengthening exercise for the gastrocnemius. With your toes pointed forward and the soles of your feet on the ground spread about hip-width apart, bend your knees so that your body

hold on to a wall or a table for stability. Slowly raise your heels off the floor until you're resting on the balls of your feet and your toes. Return the heels to the floor. Do several sets of ten repetitions. As the injured leg heals, graduate to doing the toe raises from a standing position. Finally, do the exercise standing on only one leg at a time. Do these movements regularly and frequently.

Early Treatment Is the Key

Early and aggressive treatment of tennis leg can produce fairly quick results. Many patients recover within a few weeks. A more passive approach can stretch out the recovery period to months. Once you've recovered, you need to maintain the strength in your calves, so continue doing the toe raises on a regular basis. You may also find that if the heel of your tennis shoe is low, it may stretch the Achilles tendon too much. This can be remedied by putting a 1/4-inch to 3/8-inch lift made of cork or some other shock-absorbing material into the heel of the shoe.

BLISTERS

Those new to the game of tennis or those returning after a layoff are susceptible to blisters, either on their racket hand or on their feet. Blisters, which are an accumulation of fluid between the two top layers of the skin, are caused by friction. The body's natural defense for this type of irritation is the production of callouses, but they take time to build. If you go out and play for a couple of hours on your first day, chances are good that you'll have a blister or two by the time you're done. By gradually increasing your playing time, you'll allow your skin to develop the protection it needs.

Preventing Hand Blisters

Pay attention to the contact areas between your hand and the racket handle. Make sure that the grip fits your hand properly. If it's too big or too small, the racket will tend to slip in your hand, creating more friction. Keeping the racket handle dry will help too. You may even need to wear a tennis glove or tape your hands to protect your skin.

Preventing Foot Blisters

Foot blisters can be avoided by powdering your socks and the inside of your shoes, by wearing shoes that fit your foot, and by wearing either padded socks or two or more pairs of socks to reduce the pressure on your skin.

FOOT CARE

As your contact with the ground and the bones and tissues through which the momentum and force of your body is transferred, your feet are crucial to your enjoyment of tennis. Taking care of them will do as much for your game as practicing your strokes, because without their faithful service, you won't be able to get to those shots.

There are, in general, three types of feet. Those blessed with neutral feet distribute their weight evenly on both the inside and outside of the heel and forefoot. Those that roll their heels and soles to the outside and often have high arches are said to have supinated feet. Those that roll their heels and soles inward have pronated feet. The latter may have problems with sore arches and unstable ankles, especially during or after long matches.

A myriad of ailments can afflict your feet, including sprains, sore arches, heel pain, black or tennis toe (caused by constant pressure on the big toe), athlete's foot, metatarsalgia (pain in the ball or forefoot), bunions and hammertoes (pain in the smaller toes that is often accompanied by corns or calluses), to name a few. Depending on the degree of pain you experience from any of these, they can be treated with ice and relieved by rest and choosing proper footwear. The latter may include the use of orthotics, which are shoe inserts custom-molded to fit your feet in order to correct structural imbalances.

A LITTLE HISTORY

While it may feel to some as if tennis started with "Big" Bill Tilden and Helen "Little Miss Poker Face" Wills, the king and queen of the courts during the first half of the 1900s, the game actually has roots that date back as far as the Odyssey. Homer writes of a certain princess who batted a ball back and forth with her handmaidens. Persians were also said to enjoy a game involving long paddles and a ball and played inside an enclosed structure.

Tennis as we recognize it today originated in France under the moniker of *jeu de paume*, or game of the hand. *Tenez,* the imperative form of the French verb *tenir* (to hold), was a call used by the server and evolved into the English version of tennis. The excitement of and interest in the game was infectious from the beginning, even to the point of distraction. In 1245 the archbishop of Rouen had to ban priests from playing the game because they were neglecting their monastic duties!

A Popular Sport From the Beginning

Passion for the game evolved elsewhere as well. France's King Louis X overextended himself in a match and died from the resulting pneumonia. Charles the XIII took a fatal blow to the head from the regulation ball of the time, heavy wool wrapped inside leather. In the mid-1300's, England's Edward III had a court built inside his palace. Within 30 years, the sport outstripped archery as the national pastime, much to the dismay of Edward IV, who banned his subjects from playing. In France, the sport became the favorite of gamblers and the heavy wagering on matches grew so out of hand by the early 1600s that public exhibitions were outlawed.

Jeu de paume, also known as *court tennis* or *real tennis*, was not tennis as we know it today. The cloth or hair-filled balls required a hard surface on which to play in order to generate any bounce. Rackets were made of wood and netted with gut. Games were played indoors with a net or fringed rope of varying heights bisecting the court.

Major Wingfield's Advance

Credit for the modern, outdoor version of tennis goes to England's Major Walter Clopton Wingfield, who introduced lawn tennis, with a bouncier rubber ball, in 1873. Played outdoors, the game provided a diversion for those bored with croquet and featured an hourglass-shaped court that expanded from its width of 21 feet at the net in midcourt to 30 feet wide at the baseline. The net rose four feet eight inches above the ground, 20 inches higher than the modern standard.

Within a year, rulesmakers voided the hourglass configuration and replaced it with a rectangle measuring 78 feet long. For singles play, the width was standardized at 27 feet, with an extra nine feet added for doubles. By 1884, the net's height at midpoint was standardized at three feet.

As in earlier times, the sport's popularity proved surprising. Instead of the masses, however, tennis became the sport of the upper class, an image it has only recently begun to shake. Princes, princesses, dukes, marquises, earls, countesses, viscounts, barons and assorted other barons and knights purchased their lawn tennis kits from Major Wingfield shortly after he put them into production.

A year after Major Wingfield's innovation, the game had also made its way to Bermuda, where a vacationing Miss Mary Ewing Outerbridge of Staten Island, New York, saw a match being played. She purchased a net and a set of racquets and balls and brought the game to the Staten Island Cricket and Baseball Club.

Birth of a Tradition

While tennis was taking hold in the colonies, back in Mother England another development, one that still has enormous impact on the sport, was beginning. The All England Croquet Club, located a few minutes by train outside London in Wimbledon, installed lawn tennis into its agenda in hopes of raising its flagging fortunes. Prompted by member Henry Jones, the club sponsored an open men's tournament in 1877. *The Field*, a sporting magazine, put up a silver challenge cup worth 25 guineas as a prize and the most enduring, if not most prestigious, tennis tournament was born. Every June, the sporting world focuses its attention on the grass courts of Wimbledon, which forms the cornerstone of tennis' big four annual tournaments. The other three are the French, American and Australian Opens.

The Lore of Love and
Other Historical Anecdotes

Tennis, to the uninitiated, has some baffling nomenclature and customs. What, for example, is meant by *love*? And why are points scored in increments of 15 rather than single digits? Some, but not all, of the answers to these and other questions are available through historical reference.

We know, for example, that love corresponds to the French *l'oeuf* or egg. Besides adding a romantic tinge to the sport, love denotes zero, or, in the vernacular of the British and Americans respectively, a duck or goose egg.

Service With a Smile

The term *service* seems straightforward enough, meaning that one player serves the ball up to the other. According to Richard Schickel in his book, *The World of Tennis*, however, the term service actually originated in Henry VIII's time when he and his fellow English lords would have a servant throw the ball up in the air for them at the beginning of play.

Not as much light can be shed on the scoring system, the roots of which may touch astrology or be related to the 15-minute tolling segments of tower clocks. Attempts have been made to alter the scoring system, but have produced as much, if not more, confusion than they eliminated. James Van Alen of Newport, Rhode Island, for example, created his Van Alen Simplified Scoring System (VASSS) in the 1960s. The acronym alone foreshadowed difficulties and Van Alen's various experiments proved, in some cases, to be counterproductive. To his credit, however, he did devise a system for resolving ties. Instead of dragging on interminably, sets knotted at 6-6 can now be decided by a best of twelve "overtime" game where the winner has to win by at least two points.

Tasty Bisque

And just in case you thought bisque referred only to soup, you may find it intriguing that the term can apply to tennis as well. For those who like to handicap their games, a *bisque* is an extra point that can be awarded at any time during a match. If, for example, one player has a bisque and gains the advantage, he can redeem his bisque and win the game. A certain number of bisques could be allotted before the match and the handicapped player can use them at his discretion.

A Gripping Tale

You might also think that holding the racket would be a simple affair. You just pick the darned thing up and swing away. Open any book on tennis instruction, however, and you'll see references to a variety of clasping methods, all of which contain geographical references. There are the Eastern forehand and backhand grip, the Continental grip and the Western grip. Each calls for slightly different placement of the hand on the racket grip and can be used most effectively for certain shots. The Western grip, for example, works best to catch fast moving balls hit on hard surfaces, such as the concrete courts so popular in the western United States.

The Tennis Court Oath

Although many might think that the *tennis court oath* refers to one's reaction to a missed overhead return or an opponent's blistering forehand passing shot, the term actually dates back to the French Revolution. In 1789, the sport of court tennis had lost its appeal in the face of the revolution that was sweeping Gaul. However, one jeu de paume court in Versailles did provide a meeting place for the partisans after they were locked out of their usual digs. At that meeting, the constituents took their tennis court oath, vowing not to disband until the revolution was successful. Not much later, the sport itself was banned by the revolutionaries. The court at Versailles still survives as a museum to their struggle.

The Last Emperor's Last Match

Many tennis players have been interrupted on the court to attend to an emergency, be it a crying child or a broken water main. Such disasters hardly compare, however, to the mixed doubles match in progress within China's Forbidden City in 1911. News arrived during play that one of its participants, Emperor Pu-Yi ("The Last Emperor"), had been overthrown, thus ending almost 300 years of the Manchu Dynasty. Presumably, no one asked the former head of state if he'd like to take the point over!

More Than a Tennis Match

While most of us recall the track star Jesse Owens and his success in 1936 against Hitler's Aryan athletes, the Olympic Stadium was not the only venue in which pre-World War II political drama was played out. In 1937, California's Don Budge met Germany's Baron Gottfried von Cramm in the pivotal match of the Davis Cup, the annual international men's team tennis competition. Tall, blond and blue eyed, von Cramm may have embodied the Nazi ideal, but he himself was no fan of the dictator's policies.

Just prior to taking Centre Court at Wimbledon, von Cramm received a phone call from "der Fuhrer," who exhorted von Cramm to triumph for the Fatherland. Budge recalls that his opponent came onto the court with a most serious look on his face and a frantic intensity to his game. The match, which has been described as one of the greatest of the century, ended almost four hours later when Budge lunged to hit a searing forehand passing shot that the German was unable to answer. The latter was eventually arrested by the Gestapo and sent to a concentration camp.

Royalty on the Court

King Gustav V of Sweden first travelled to England as a 20-year-old in 1878. Part of his training as a future monarch included acquainting himself with the institutions and customs of another country, and from England he brought home a love for tennis. In succeeding years, "Papa Gustav" popularized the sport in his homeland and entered tournaments on the French Riviera under the name of "Mr. G." Tennis remained an integral part of his life, which eventually spanned 92 years. Perhaps his devotion to the sport aided his vitality. As an octegenarian, he was described as being as active as a man thirty years his junior. And after a successful operation in 1942, his doctor proclaimed that the king "had a heart like a boy's."

Serving Up a New Generation of Women Players

The emergence of women and their influence on the tennis world preceeded the current rise of female politicians. The power that women are enjoying in both arenas is nevertheless sweetly cherished. In 1990, Patti Murray of Washington State was told by a state legislator that she would never wield any influence because she was "just a housewife in tennis shoes." Upon her election to the U.S. Senate in 1992, Ms. Murray presented her rubberized footwear to the world as a indication of how far she and her sisters have come.

THE RULES OF THE GAME

The Court

Tennis is played on a rectangular court measuring 78 feet long by 27 feet wide for singles and 36 feet wide for doubles. The net bisects the rectangle and measures three feet at its center and six inches higher on each end. The lines marking the ends of the court are called baselines. The service lines, which are 21 feet away from the net, and the center service line, which bisects the service lines, form four boxes inside the court. These are known as the service courts.

Choosing Service

Singles games involve one player on each side of the net. The competitors choose who will serve first. A popular method is for one player to spin his racket and let it fall on the ground. The other player, without looking, calls out whether the racket's trademark on the butt end of the handle landed right side up or down. If the call is correct, the player who made the call gets to serve or receive first or to choose which side of the court he would like to play on. If the call is incorrect, the player who spun his racket gets to choose his preference. You can make up your own variations of this process (and save wear on your racket!) by using a coin toss, for example.

Serving the Ball

The game begins with the server standing behind the baseline and between the center mark and the right singles sideline. The server gets two chances to hit the ball into the service court diagonally opposite of his position, which is the receiver's right hand service court. After the point has been played, the server moves to the left of the center mark and serves to his opponent's other service court. The server continues alternating sides after each point throughout the game.

The server should not step on or inside of the baseline before striking the ball. The motion of the serve may draw the server's feet off the ground, which is allowed as long as their foot or feet don't land on or inside the baseline until after the ball has been hit. Violation of this rule is called a foot fault, and the offender is charged with an unsuccessful serve.

If the server's ball hits the top of the net and bounces over into proper service court, a *let* serve is called and the server takes the shot over. If the server misses, a *fault* is called. If the server misses both serves, he has *double faulted* and loses the point.

The receiver can stand wherever he wants on his side of the court. He must return the ball after one bounce and can hit it anywhere in the server's court. On the service and for all other exchanges, a ball that touches a line is considered good. Unless you have an umpire calling balls in and out, the players themselves must make the calls. In most cases, players call balls out on their side of the net. Silence after a shot bounces once indicates that the ball landed in the court and the other player will attempt to return it.

Scoring Points

A player scores points when his opponent hits the ball outside of the court or into the net, or if he fails to make a return before the ball bounces twice. After the serve, both players may hit the ball in the air before it lands in their court. A player may not, however, touch the ball before it crosses the net, nor may he touch the net with his racket, hand, feet or body. Doing so results in the automatic loss of the point.

A player can also lose a point by:

- throwing his racket at the ball
- deliberately catching or carrying the ball on the racket strings
- touching the ball with anything other than their racket during play

- hindering his opponent while he is making a shot
- touching or catching the ball during a point even if he's standing outside the court.

The last point requires a little explanation. If your opponent hits a ball that is going out, let it go. If you hit the ball or catch it, or if it hits you, your opponent can claim that the shot would have landed inside the lines. This is a rule that is not likely to cause trouble between friends or long time opponents, but there are times in tennis when players will take advantage of every nuance they can lay their hands on.

Scoring a Game

A game is played in a succession of points. The traditional scoring system does not, however, increase by any logical mathematical sequence. Winner of the first point earns a score of 15. If the server wins the first point, for example, the score is 15-love. (Love, as is sometimes the case in life, means much but stands for zero points). The next point raises the score to 30, followed by 40. If the score is tied at 40-all, also called deuce, the players must continue until someone wins by two points. The player who wins the first point after deuce is said to have the advantage. If the advantaged player loses the next point, the score goes back to deuce and the players try again to win by two. Deuce games can go on for awhile.

Various informal phrases are used to indicate some of the above deuce situations. The advantaged player may say "My ad" or "Ad here" to indicate the score. If the server holds the advantage, the phrase "Ad in" may be used. If the receiver has the edge, the phrase is "Ad out."

Changing Sides

After the first game, the player who received for the first game serves. Service continues to alternate after every game. Also following completion of the first game, players traditionally change sides to negate any advantages one side of the court may have over the other, such as glaring sun, wind or a background that makes the ball hard to see. Thereafter, players change sides every other game. An easy way to remember this is that you switch whenever the sum of the games played adds up to an odd number, such as 1-0, 2-1, 4-3 or 5-4.

Scoring a Set

To win the set, one player must win at least six games and be ahead by at least two games. If the set is tied after six games, the players can employ a tie breaker. One method is to play a best of 12 points game where the points add up by ones. The first player to reach seven wins as long as he is at least two points ahead. If the tie breaker reaches a score of 7-6 or 7-all, play continues until one player pulls ahead by two.

Breaking a Tie

Serving in the 12-point tie breaker gets a bit complex. Service still alternates between the two players as it did during the set, but the first server serves only one point from the right hand, or deuce, court. The serve then goes to the other player, who starts play from the left, or ad, court and serves two points. Serve then goes back to the original server, who starts play from the left court and serves for another two points. This pattern continues until six points have been played, at which time the players change sides for another six points. Again this procedure continues until the game has been concluded.

Another tie breaking method is to play a sudden death game where the first player to reach five points, for example, wins, even if he ends up with only one more point than his opponent. This no-ad scoring method can also be used throughout a set and is employed in situations where time restrictions are important. A no-ad game would be played in a simple succession of single points — 1-2-3-game.

Rules for Doubles

The rules for playing doubles are basically the same as for singles. The service courts are the same, but once the ball has been put in play by the server, the ball can be returned anywhere inside the baseline and the doubles sidelines. Doubles players have a wider area in which to hit the ball and a larger area to cover than in singles.

The serving sequence in doubles calls for partners to alternate their service. One partner will serve the entire first game and the other will serve the third game. When receiving service, each player is responsible for one side of the court and only the player opposite the server may return the service. After that initial exchange, either player on both sides of the net may hit the ball back.

After the first set, teammates may decide to change the order in which they serve. The player who served first in the first set may now serve second, but once the pattern is established, it must be maintained throughout the set.

With two players swinging away at the ball, there are times when one will tick the ball slightly. His partner, unaware perhaps that contact was made, will catch up to the ball and make the return. Fairness dictates, however, that the player who ticked the ball acknowledge that fact and awards the point to his opponents. If, on the other hand, one player takes a mighty swing and misses completely, his partner can back him up and make the return before the ball bounces twice. The only time one player can't back up the other, as mentioned earlier, is on the service.

A Worldwide Sport

All these rules have been developed and refined over many years. They work well for the majority of the sport's participants, and they provide a common language for tennis players all over the world. If you find yourself on a tiny atoll in the Marshall Islands, for example, with a racket and a ball, you can pick up a friendly game with one of the locals (many of whom do, in fact, enjoy tennis) and know how to keep score.

Alternative Scoring Methods

Of course, no one says you have to play by the rules. Creative variations can be employed for fun and practice. In their book *Use Your Head In Tennis*, authors Bob Harman and Keith Monroe describe a game called *ghost doubles*, whereby two players can reduce the court area to practice their doubles play or to make the game less physically demanding. To play the game, the server sends the ball into the opponent's service court, as he would normally. The player making the return, however, can only send the ball back to the side of the court from which the server initiated play. For the rest of the point, a shot is only good if it lands on the half of the court diagonally opposite the player hitting the ball. It's as if there were a "ghost" covering the other half of each player's court.

Rules for games can also be less oriented towards winning and losing. In his book *The*

Tiddling Tennis Theorem, Art Hoppe describes a fictional tennis instructor, called the Professor, who expounds the philosophical notion that tennis is essentially absurd. At one point, the Professor and his love interest, Miss Merribuck, retire to a sequestered court and engage in their own, Zen-like version of the game which they call cooperative tennis. Afterwards, the Professor tries to explain what they were doing to another member of the tennis club:

"You see, in cooperative tennis, the idea is to hit the ball over the net within the lines as many times as possible. When one of us hits it over, it's a victory for both of us. When one of us fails, it's defeat for both of us. But we succeeded far more often than we failed, so both of us won, don't you see?" (Reprinted with permission of the author.)

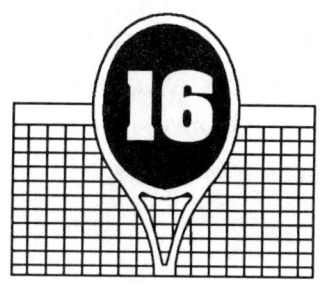

TENNIS ETIQUETTE

Tennis prides itself as a civilized sport. In addition to the codified rules of the sport, there also exists a body of unwritten rules that are, for the most part, followed by players throughout the world. This code of conduct adheres to the basic tenents of good sportsmanship and the golden rule — "Do unto other players what you would want them to do to you."

There are, of course, those among the professional ranks who have built reputations on defying some of these guidelines and have become quite famous in the process. Their antics received more attention than they warranted, unfortunately, and they no doubt inspired others to mimic their behavior. Take comfort in the fact that unsportsmanlike players, whether they act belligerently, engage in extreme gamesmanship or cheat outright, are wrestling with internal demons that are far more frightening than any player they will ever face across the net.

Common sense will get you through most situations not covered in the rules. As an aid to some particular situations or protocols, here are some of the unwritten rules of tennis:

Clothing

Tennis whites used to be mandatory for play on some courts, and may still be at certain locales. The color barrier, if you will, has been broken in recent years, and clothing of a variety of hues is now acceptable. Form follows function with regard to what you wear: shorts, a pullover shirt and rubber-soled tennis shoes. Individual clubs or resorts may have their own restrictions, which you should check before you start play (or arrive for your vacation!).

Entering the Court

When walking to your court, disturb other players as little as possible. If you have to cross a court where people are playing, wait until they either wave you across or they end the point in progress.

Warming Up Before a Match

When warming up, concentrate on hitting balls to your rival rather than away from him so that you can both get prepared. Some players will ask for a selection of shots, including groundstrokes, serves, volleys and overheads to get themselves ready. An acceptable warm-up time before a set is around 10 to 15 minutes.

Ball Maintenance

The server should have at least two balls in his possession at the start of each point. Some players hold the extra ball in their nonracket hand while playing. Others tuck the ball into a pocket, under their shorts or on a special holder that fits on the back of a belt. The reason to have the second ball ready is so that if you miss your first serve, you can quickly prepare for the second serve without chasing around the court for another ball.

If the first serve misses and ends up in the playing area on either side of the net, you can (and should, for safety reasons) retrieve the ball so that the court is clear. If someone else's ball enters your court while you're in the middle of a point, you should stop play so that no one unknowingly trips over the ball. If you were in the middle of a game, start over again with the first serve and replay the point.

The receiver calls the serve in or out. Traditionally, you loudly say "Out" if the shot was no good — if it landed outside the lines of the service court. If you say nothing, the server can assume that his shot was good and will expect you to return the ball.

You are responsible for calling balls on your side of the net. Any benefit of the doubt should go to your opponent, but if you clearly see that his shot was out, then you should call it as such. If your opponent isn't sure if your shot landed in or out on his side of the net, he can ask you for your opinion. If you were unable to see the ball clearly, then you can both agree to play the point over. It's considered bad form to ask a third party (unless that person is an umpire whose duty it is to referee your play) to make a call.

Talking During Play

Refrain from talking during match play, other than to indicate if a ball was out or to communicate with your partner in doubles (such as "I've got it," or "You take it"). Don't distract your opponent, or have friends try to cheer you on, when the ball is in play.

Keeping Track of the Score

The server should announce the set score, starting with his score first (for example, "four-two" or "four serving two") before each game and the game score (for example, "thirty-forty") before serving each point. Sometimes you will forget the score, in which case you can either reconstruct the game and/or set until you both agree or go back to the last score that you remember being correct.

Rules for Court Play

Know the rules for play that apply to the court on which you're playing. If there are others waiting to use the court, you may be limited to a specific time, such as one hour, or a specific number of sets before you must yield the court to someone else.

Compliments and Encouragement

Kind words, to your opponent, your doubles partner and yourself, will do more for your enjoyment of the game than disparaging remarks. If your rival makes a good shot, compliment him. If your partner is struggling, encourage him. If you lose a game or a match, acknowledge that your opponent played a better game. Savor your good shots and think dispassionately about what you can do to improve. Realize that winning means more than the final score. Resolve to do better next time, and rejoice in the fact that there will be a next time.

Make tennis your lifetime sport!

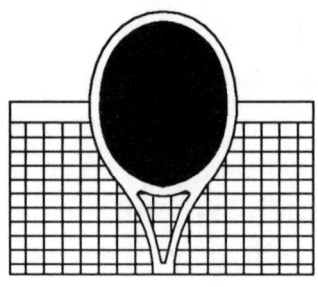

RESOURCES

NATIONAL TENNIS ORGANIZATIONS

- **US Tennis Association**
  70 West Red Oak Lane
  White Plains, NY 10604
  914-696-7000

  Provides an umbrella organization for competitive and recreational tennis in the U.S. Has special committees for recreational, senior, sports science and technical aspects of the game. The association also produces a catalog of publications and videos, and the *USTA Basic 10 Flexibility Exercises* on a laminated card.

- **National Senior Women's Tennis Association**
  Irene Higbee, President
  205 Belhaven Ave.
  Linwood, NJ 08221
  609-927-6673

  Promotes competitive tennis for players 30 and older.

- **Super-Senior Tennis, Inc.**
  John Powless, Secretary/Treasurer
  PO Box 44715
  Madison, WI 53744
  608-274-6262

  Promotes tennis for players 55 and older.

- **John Subrizi Senior Tennis Program**
  309 Thunder Hill Drive
  Stamford, CT 06902
  203-322-2706

  Offers free tennis instruction for players over 50.

- **American Medical Tennis Association** (AMTA)
  Bill Drake, Exec. Director
  P.O. Box 841 Alton, IL 62002
  618-462-6841

  Promotes tennis among physicians and their families.

- **American Tennis Association (ATA)**
  P.O. Box 3277
  Silver Spring, MD 20901
  301-681-4832

  Promotes interest in tennis, especially among African-Americans.

- **United States Dental Tennis Association**
  Sue Ballantyne, Exec. Secretary
  7320 Southwest Arbor Lake Drive
  Wilsonville, OR 97070
  503-694-2524

  Encourages dentists to play tennis.

- **United States Recreational Tennis Association (USRTA)**
  Otto Bernath, President
  3112 Adderley Ct.
  Silver Spring, MD 20906
  301-598-4820

  Promotes recreational tennis using the U.S. Handicap Rating System.

- **National Public Parks Tennis Association (NPPTA)**
  Hollis Smith, Exec. Director
  3325 Wilshire Blvd., Suite 604
  Los Angeles, CA 90010
  213-380-7114

  Programs for tennis at public parks.

- **National Tennis Academy (NTA)**
  Joe Cockerham, Director
  P.O. Box N, Suite 104
  Waxahachie, TX 75165
  214-937-0311

  Trains and certifies tennis instructors.

- **People-To-People Tennis Committee (PPTC)**
  P.O. Box 2650
  La Jolla, CA 92038
  619-459-3393

  Organizes overseas tennis matches trips for senior players, who act as goodwill ambassadors.

ADDITIONAL SENIOR SPORTS AND HEALTH ASSOCIATIONS

- **President's Council on Physical Fitness and Sports**
  Suite 250, 701 Pennsylvania Ave NW Washington, DC 20004 202-272-3421

- **National Recreation and Park Association (NRPA)**
  2775 South Quincy St., Suite 300
  Arlington, VA 22206
  703-820-4940

- **The National Council on the Aging, Inc.**
  409 Third St. SW, Suite 200
  Washington, DC 20024
  202-479-1200

- **American Alliance for Health, Physical Education, Recreation and Dance**
  Ray Ciszek, Vice President
  1900 Association Drive
  Reston, VA 22091
  703-476-3431

- **National Association of Governor's Councils on Physical Fitness and Sports**
  Pan American Plaza
  201 S. Capitol Ave, Suite 560
  Indianapolis, IN 46225
  317-237-5630

- **American Association of Retired Persons (AARP)**
  601 E Street N.W.
  Washington, D.C. 20049

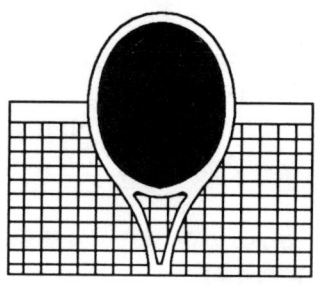

BIBLIOGRAPHY

Anderson, Bob. *Stretching*. Bolinas, CA: Shelter Publications, 1980.

Bergeron, J. David, and Holly Wilson Greene. *Coaches Guide To Sports Injuries*. Champaign, IL: Human Kinetics Books, 1989.

Block, Maxine, Editor. *Current Biography: Who's News and Why 1942*. New York, NY: H.W. Wilson, 1942.

Bollettieri, Nick. *Tennis Your Way*. North Palm Beach, FL: The Athletic Institute, 1982.

Boltin, Alan S. *Bathroom Tennis*. New York: Ballentine Books, 1978.

Brown, Jim. *Tennis: Steps to Success*. Champaign, IL: Leisure Press, 1989.

Bunis, Alvin. W., and Roger Williams. *The Tennis Grand Masters: How To Play Winning Tennis In The Prime Of Life*. Norwalk, CT: Golf Digest/Tennis, Inc., 1983.

Burwash, Peter, and John Tullius. *Peter Burwash's Tennis For Life*. New York: Times Books, 1981.

Chirls, Stuart. Sole concerns: choosing the right tread. *Tennis Magazine*, December 1992, p. 44.

Connors, Jimmy, with Neil Gordon, M.D., Ph.D., and Catherine McEvily Harris. *Don't Count Yourself Out: Staying Fit After 35*. New York: Hyperion Press, 1991.

Deutsch, Robin. Meet the man who invented the widebody. *Tennis Magazine*, February 1989, pp. 65-66.

Deutsch, Robin. How to buy a fitting shoe. *Tennis Magazine*, April 1991, pp. 102-104.

Evans, William J., M.D. How to change your biological age. *Bottom Line Personal*, 28 February 1993, pp. 13-14.

Fixx, James F. *Maximum Sports Performance*. New York: Random House, 1985.

Fonda, Jane, with Mignon McCarthy. *Women Coming Of Age*. New York: Simon And Schuster, 1984.

Forsythe, Kenneth, M.D., and Neil Feineman. *Athletics For Life: Optimal Fitness Through Recreational Sports*. New York: Simon & Schuster, Inc., 1985.

Gallwey, W. Timothy. *The Inner Game of Tennis*. New York: Random House, 1974.

Garrick, James G., M.D. with Gerald Secor Couzens. Tennis leg: how I manage gastrocnemius strains. *The Physician and Sportsmedicine*, Vol 20, No. 5, (May, 1992): pp. 203-207.

Greenberg, Jerrold S., and David Pargman. *Physical Fitness: A Wellness Approach.*, 2nd ed. Englewood Cliffs, NJ: Prentice-Hall, 1989.

Groppel, Jack L. *High Tech Tennis*, 2nd ed. Champaign, IL: Leisure Press, 1992.

Harding, Warren G., III, M.D. Use and misuse of the tennis elbow strap. *The Physician and Sportsmedicine*. Vol 20, No. 8 (August 1992): pp. 65-74.

Harman, Bob, and Keith Monroe. *Use Your Head in Tennis*, revised edition. Port Washington, NY: Kennikat Press, 1974.

Harvey, Jack, M.D., James Glick, M.D., William Stanish, M.D., and Carol Teitz, M.D. Tennis elbow: what's the best treatment? *The Physician and Sportsmedicine*. Vol 18, No.6 (June 1990): pp. 62-74.

Herman, Hank. Back pain:signal that should not be ignored. *The New York Times*, 11 February 1991, p.C10.

Hoppe, Arthur. *The Tiddling Tennis Theorem*. New York: The Viking Press, 1977.

Karnowski, Frank. Equipment check: straighten strings for uniform performance & wear. *Tennis Magazine*, October 1989, pg. 21.

Kart, Cary Steven, Eileen K. Metress and Seamus P. Metress. *Aging, Health and Society*, 2nd ed. Boston, MA: Jones and Bartlett Publishers, 1988.

King, Bille Jean, and Cynthia Starr. *We Have Come A Long Way*. San Francisco: McGraw-Hill, 1988.

Lardner, Rex. *The Complete Beginner's Guide to Tennis*. Garden City, NY: Doubleday & Company, Inc., 1967.

Mason, R. Elaine. *Tennis*. Boston: Allyn and Bacon, Inc., 1974.

Morton, Jason, and Russell Seymour with Clyde Burleson. *Winning Tennis After Forty*. Englewood Cliffs, NJ: Prentice-Hall, Inc., 1980.

Montgomery, Dr. Jim. *Tennis For The Mature Adult*. Jackson, MI: Hunter's Mountain Tennis Corporation, 1979.

Perlman, David. Exercise slashes risk of heart disease. *San Francisco Chronicle*, 25 February 1993, p. A20.

Roark, Eldon. The Super Seniors. *World Tennis Magazine*, 1975.

Schickel, Richard. *The World of Tennis*. New York: Random House, 1975.

Schwed, Peter. *Quality Tennis After 50...Or 60...Or 70...Or...* New York: St. Martin's Press, 1990.

Scott, Eugene. *Tennis: Game of Motion*. New York: Crown Publishers, Inc., 1973.

Sharnoff, David, and Susan Festa Fiske. Oh, my aching feet. *Tennis Magazine*, April 1992, pp. 70-75.

Simons, William G. The tennis and politics mixer. *Inside Tennis Magazine*, December/January 1993, p.9.

Stites, Pamela. An exercise in longevity. *World Tennis Magazine*, May, 1989, pp. 16-18.

Tutko, Thomas and William Bruns. *Winning Is Everything and Other American Myths*. New York, NY: Macmillan Publishing Co., Inc., 1976.

Tver, David F., and Howard F. Hunt. *Encyclopedic Dictionary of Sports Medicine*. New York: Chapman and Hall, 1986.

United States Tennis Association. *USTA Senior Tennis Directory*. Princeton, N.J.: United State Tennis Association/Center for Education and Recreational Tennis, 1988.

University of California, Berkeley. *The Wellness encyclopedia: the Comprehensive Family Resource for Safeguarding Health and Preventing Illness*. Boston, MA: Houghton Mifflin Co., 1991.

Vikhanski, Luba/Medical Tribune News Service. The best calorie burners. *San Francisco Chronicle*, 2 February 1993, p. B3.

Walker, Morton, D.P.M. Secrets of Los Viejos - the old ones. *Townsend Letter for Doctors*, December, 1992, pp. 174-177.

Workman, Jill. Answers to your most common string questions. *Tennis Magazine*, November 1991, pp. 74-76.

Workman, Jill. How to shop for strings. *Tennis Magazine*, March 1989, pp. 101-103.

Wright, Bill. Aerobic Tennis: *How to Get Fit and Play Better*. Bolinas, CA: Shelter Publications, Inc., 1983.

INDEX